CANCELLED

Preventing Violence in Relationships

MAIN LENDI

of related interest

Childhood Experiences of Domestic Violence
Caroline McGee
ISBN 1 85302 827 4

Domestic Violence
Guidelines for Research-Informed Practice
Edited by John P. Vincent and Ernest N. Jouriles
ISBN 1 85302 854 1

Making an Impact: Children and Domestic Violence
A Reader
Marianne Hester, Chris Pearson and Nicola Harwin
ISBN 1 85302 844 4

Good Practice in Working with Violence
Edited by Hazel Kemshall and Jacki Pritchard
ISBN 1 85302 641 7
Good Practice 6

Assessing Men who Sexually Abuse
A Practice Guide
David Briggs, Paddy Doyle, Tess Gooch and Roger Kennington
ISBN 1 85302 435 X

Violence in Children and Adolescents
Edited by Ved Varma
ISBN 1 85302 344 2

Preventing Violence in Relationships

A Programme for Men Who Feel They Have a Problem with their Use of Controlling and Violent Behaviour

Gerry Heery

Jessica Kingsley Publishers
London and Philadelphia

The pages marked with a ✓ may be photocopied for use in therapeutic programmes with violent men, but may not be reproduced for other purposes without the prior permission of the publisher.

All rights reserved. No paragraph of this publication may be reproduced, copied or transmitted save with written permission of the Copyright Act 1956 (as amended), or under the terms of any licence permitting limited copying issued by the Copyright Licensing Agency, 33-34 Alfred Place, London WC1E 7DP. Any person who does any unauthorised act in relation to this publication may be liable to prosecution and civil claims for damages.

The right of Gerry Heery to be identified as author of this work has been asserted by him in accordance with the Copyright, Designs and Patents Act 1988.

First published in the United Kingdom in 2001 by
Jessica Kingsley Publishers Ltd,
116 Pentonville Road, London
N1 9JB, England

and

325 Chestnut Street,
Philadelphia PA 19106, USA.

www.jkp.com

© Copyright 2001 Gerry Heery

Library of Congress Cataloging in Publication Data

A CIP catalog record for this book is available from the Library of Congress

British Library Cataloguing in Publication Data

A CIP catalogue record for this book is available from the British Library

ISBN 1 85302 816 9

Printed and Bound in Great Britain by
Athenaeum Press, Gateshead, Tyne and Wear

616.858220651 HEE

03005415X

Contents

The following symbols have been used throughout the book:

 Worksheet

 Overhead

 photocopiable page

To Maire, who has supported, encouraged and challenged me
to complete this project. I will always be deeply grateful.

'When you love you open your life to another'

Acknowledgements

This publication has been a personal initiative. I have received much encouragement and support from a number of individuals to whom I am grateful and in particular, I would like to thank the following:

Rita Glover, Robin McRoberts and the Belfast Relate team, including the admin. staff. Their encouragement, support and advice were critical in allowing me to make a start on the programme in early 1999. My sincere thanks to Margie Houston, who took the time to observe some of the sessions and give me her feedback on the process. She has also been energetic in advocating the programme within her organisation.

Angela Courtney, Northern Ireland's Women's Aid Federation, who has been positive about the programme and has continued to offer support and direct me to resources. Also many thanks to Deirdre Teague and Carol of the Help Line.

Special thanks to Margot Hesketh and Noelle Collins of Belfast Women's Aid. Margot has offered me consultation and support, allowing me to continue to move forward with the project. Her practical advice through difficult times has been invaluable. Noelle has facilitated the sessions for participants' wives and partners in a very sensitive and helpful way.

Joan McGovern of Barnardo's, who has listened, advised and sought to promote the programme.

Father Michael McGinnity who has also spread the word along with Deirdre O'Rawe of Accord, Northern Ireland.

Margaret Fawcett of the Social Work department at Queen's University (and Relate), who has been positive and active in supporting the programme and particularly in setting up an evaluation process.

Finally, I would like to acknowledge the vision, dedication, and commitment of those many people who have pioneered this work long before my involvement, and who continue to practise. In putting together this programme, I researched several others. These included the Duluth, Emerge (America), as well as the Change, Lothian Domestic Violence Probation Project (LDVPP), and Men Overcoming Violence (MOVE) programmes in Britain and Ireland. (I have referenced these programmes in the text.)

Introduction

It is to be hoped that, as you are reading this, the difficult peace process in Northern Ireland is continuing to struggle towards the creation of a more stable, acceptable and peaceful society. However, one of the results of the reduction in levels of political instability and violence has been the increased awareness of other serious problems which have tended to remain hidden. One clear example of this has been the presence of domestic violence. In 1998, ten people, eight women and two men, died in Northern Ireland as a result of domestic violence (Dept of Economic Development 1999). There were also high levels of recorded incidents involving serious injury, and again the large majority of victims were women. In addition, there are many unrecorded occasions of domestic violence (McWilliams and Spence 1996). Such figures show that a proportionately more serious problem exists than in other comparable locations, although given the concealed nature of the subject, it is difficult to speak about it with absolute authority.

There is an abundance of local, national and international research to indicate the existence of controlling and abusive behaviours against women within relationships. This behaviour has been shown to be endemic and prevalent in all continents, cutting across racial, cultural and economic development lines. American research has identified domestic violence as women's number one health problem (Nasher and Mehrtens 1993). In Britain several recent surveys into the most serious concerns of women and children have put domestic violence at the top of the list (Worthington 1998). It is also clear that such behaviour can often escalate if it is not addressed at an early stage. The extent of the abuse and violence perpetrated on women is such that it has a 'staggering impact on individuals, families, social institutions and the society as a whole' (Edleson and Tolman 1992, p.7).

It is not just in Northern Ireland, with its unique history and circumstances, that there has been a slow and limited response to the issue of domestic violence. It was only in 1992 that the United Nations declared violence against women and children to be a human rights issue. The Council of Europe followed in 1994 with the formation of a Committee on Violence against Women. This has sought to encourage and put pressure on member states to acknowledge abuse of women as a major area of serious and continual crime. There have also been a range of regional and national developments, in recognition of the need for movement across a number of fronts if real progress is to be made.

These include:

- co-ordinated community-wide responses
- tougher and more consistent law enforcement reflecting the criminal nature of much of the behaviour
- more realistic sentencing
- relevant services for victims – refuges, support and various community safety measures
- major educational and public-awareness raising campaigns
- programmes aimed at getting abusive men to address their behaviour.

While there are signs of positive movement, much remains to be done. 'The tide may be beginning to turn but plenty of women are still drowning' (Mullender 1996, p.18).

Preventing Violence in Relationships (PVR) is a new preventative and educational programme. It has been specifically designed to be of assistance to men in hetero-sexual relationships who feel they have a problem with their use of controlling, violent and aggressive behaviours within these relationships.

This programme places itself within the above continuum, as one small part of the ongoing response to the complex problem of domestic violence. It is part of a range of measures coming from various statutory, political, voluntary and community organisations and groupings. They are all seeking in various ways and at different levels to make a positive contribution towards the better treatment of women within society. The programme has been taken forward in Northern Ireland with the encouragement of organisations working with people who are having problems as a result of domestic violence. Primarily this has involved Women's Aid, Relate, Barnardo's and Accord and other counselling services.

The starting-point with any endeavour in life is to be clear about the principles and values that give it drive and direction (Chapter 1). PVR is aimed at men who recognise that they have a problem and now want seriously to address their behaviours. It is an educational approach that will explore and challenge participants on their beliefs. It will encourage them to reflect on how they see the world and how this may go hand in hand with their abuse. It will seek to challenge and re-educate participants to begin to change the way they look at things.

The PVR programme fits within the vital context of prevention, protection and provision referred to above. It advocates zero tolerance of any violence within relationships and will do nothing that conflicts with seeking to ensure the safety of women and children. Men who commit acts of violence within their relationships need to be clear that such behaviour is unacceptable and may be dealt with through the process of the law. The PVR programme is not offered to men as a way to avoid being held accountable for their criminal behaviour.

The PVR programme has been designed in the light of relevant knowledge and the latest research. This suggests reasons as to why this type of behaviour takes place, and what may be helpful to those seeking to change long-established patterns of behaviour. I will explore what we know about the types of men who use controlling behaviours and the range of propositions put forward to explain the prevalence of such problems across all societies, past and present (Chapters 2 and 4).

The theory upon which the actual programme is based, the skills required to deliver it, and how it seeks to tackle the root causes of men's use of violent behaviour will be outlined in detail (Chapter 3).

Part II outlines the three stages of the programme, with full contents of all 26 sessions and accompanying overheads, exercises, facilitators' notes, etc. (Chapters 5, 6, 7). The programme is designed for delivery within a group but can be presented individually if required. The sessions are self-explanatory and detailed notes are provided as well as references for further reading.

As the programme is mainly educational in nature it can be delivered by anyone with a commitment to the value-base set out in the first chapter, and with sufficient skills in using the approaches and models outlined in Part I. This manual is presented as an accessible tool which can be used by committed and experienced workers across a range of settings, including social workers, counsellors, therapists, probation officers, and youth and community workers. It will assist them in encouraging the men with whom they are working to address directly their use of abusive and controlling behaviours in a structured and significant way.

Finally, in thinking about and planning this initiative I have listened to the views of women who have been abused and also to women offering services to these victims. A significant number of victims have expressed a strong need for some form of intervention that may have a positive impact on their partners' behaviour. They have indicated that they want their relationships to continue but the abuse to stop. Some women also remarked with regret that if only something had been done earlier, then things might not have been so bad.

The PVR programme is primarily directed at the men who need to do the work. It offers something constructive but challenging to those who are motivated to address their use of abusive and controlling behaviours. It is not about making false promises and raising unrealistic expectations. It can only be one small part of a much broader solution and it will not be relevant in all situations. However, it can offer a concrete and direct response to those men who are beginning to recognise that they have a problem to deal with and are sufficiently motivated to take on the difficult work of change.

PART I

The Foundation of Practice

The Value, Knowledge and Skills Base

1

Principles for Practice

Domestic violence is a complex and fraught area. It involves a wide range of behaviours, from verbal and emotional abuse to physical attacks which cause serious injury and possibly death. It is therefore a matter for both the civil and criminal law working together with many different agencies.

As already indicated, it requires multi-faceted legal responses and systematic and comprehensive approaches (Coomaraswamy 1998). Within this positive context it is important that preventative and educational approaches are developed and made widely available. However, interventions such as the PVR programme should be brought forward with care, and in alignment with the following package of underpinning values.

Zero Tolerance of Domestic Violence

If women are to be protected, then it is critical that domestic violence is recognised as a serious problem. Difficulties arise when it is ignored, played down, or seen to be a private matter; 'When it is not acknowledged that such traumatic events go on day and daily behind closed doors of family homes' (McWilliams and McKiernan 1993, p.6). The criminal nature of domestic violence behaviour needs to be recognised. The symbolic and denunciatory relevance of the law relating to domestic violence is important. Men who commit serious and violent offences against women should be duly processed and made responsible for their behaviour.

Enhancing the Safety and Protection of Women

Within any intervention, no action should be taken which puts a woman in danger. If there are concerns about a particular woman's safety, then these should be addressed (See Chapter 4). On a more general level and in the long run, it will only be possible to make significant contributions to enhancing women's safety through positive changes in the men who use these behaviours. The PVR programme seeks to help participants make changes in their violent behaviour. Through this it will seek to reduce the pain and distress caused to women and children.

Personal Responsibility and Accountability for Behaviour

Individuals need to take full responsibility and to be accountable for their behaviour. To be responsible for what he has done, a man needs to begin to understand the full consequences of his actions for his wife or partner and children. He then needs to face up fully to his behaviour and its effects (Zehr 1995). Furthermore, he should participate in finding ways to see how things can be made right and the extent to which this is possible. This may involve him in having to make significant changes in his behaviour and he may also have to accept his partner's view that their relationship is now over.

Change is Possible

Change is difficult for all of us. 'If we don't have to change we don't' (Egan 1995, p.78). This is particularly true for men who have deeply established patterns of abusive and controlling behaviour. These may have been learned within their own families as children and reinforced over many years by various experiences within their wider community and society. The deep-rooted nature of violence and abuse against women requires the wider co-ordinated response already referred to. The process of real change needs to be addressed at different levels. There needs to be a conjunction of justice, confrontation, support and motivation (Mullender 1996). However, within this context, the PVR programme seeks to offer those men who are motivated to change, the opportunity for structured support and challenge. It will help take them through the process of change which 'can be slow, difficult and deliberate' (Covey 1992, p.32). It requires hard, honest self-examination – a willingness to be brutally honest about a lifestyle that has hurt other people. It is my belief that ultimately some men can, over a considerable period of time, make positive changes.

Programme Effectiveness

As part of a wide range of alternative responses to domestic violence, the PVR programme seeks to play a small but significant part in facilitating participants to make positive and long-lasting changes in their behaviours and their lives. To do this, it is committed to striving for the best possible practice. It is about delivering something that is effective. The programme has been designed with clear objectives and a definite rationale. It follows research that suggests that it is possible for people to change. This is a relatively new area of work, which is innovative and constantly evolving as new research emerges. Quality matters, and the key is to maintain a commitment to a quality product, delivered with integrity, and to continue to experiment, develop and improve (Daft 1995).

Value Dilemmas

From time to time, situations may arise which cause tensions and dilemmas within the above values. For example, a participant may disclose details of violent behaviour against his wife. In terms of zero tolerance, the immediate view may be to ask the man to withdraw from the course. In addition, if there is sufficient detail about a possible criminal offence the decision may be taken to report it to the police so that he can be held accountable. However, the man's partner may then indicate that such a course of action may endanger her safety and that she does not want to pursue a matter which happened some time ago. Or she may indicate that she feels her partner is benefiting from the programme and withdrawal may put an end to her hopes for change.

There can be no hard and fast rules in this area of work. It is important to recognise the uniqueness of each situation, to address it and seek to respond flexibly and appropriately to the various circumstances that are present. 'Pragmatism, and ensuring that we achieve our purpose, come before rigid ideology' (Lloyd 1996, p.18). To this end, the core purpose that needs to be kept in mind is to ensure that the protection and safety of women is of paramount importance. In line with criminal justice based programmes, no action should be taken which in the view of a woman would put her safety in jeopardy (Morran and Wilson 1999). These issues will be discussed further in Chapter 4.

Conclusion

The PVR programme has positioned itself at the preventative, educational end of the continuum of our community's emerging response to domestic violence. A clear value-base has been outlined upon which the programme rests. In the following chapters I shall explore how this base is brought to life and integrated into the knowledge and skill areas involved in designing an appropriate and effective preventative intervention.

2
Understanding Domestic Violence

Introduction

The nature and causes of various forms of violence have been the subject of much study over many years. Attempts to explain violence are to be found in many fields, including religion, philosophy, psychology, sociology, anthropology, politics and genetics. The study of the particular issue of the use of violence by men against women within close relationships, although encompassed in some of the wider studies, has a relatively shorter history. This chapter will briefly overview some of the approaches, insights and findings from research which have been put forward to try to explain such behaviour. Researchers and academics have delved into genetic, psychological and social processes in seeking to explain the decision of some men to use violence within their relationships. One helpful way to organise this material is to look separately at each of these three areas (see Fig. 2.1).

Genetic Factors

There has been a long history of research into the biological and genetic make-up of individuals in terms of seeking to explain certain aspects of their behaviour. The key question is whether there are identifiable influences arising from genetic factors that may assist in understanding why some men are violent to their female partners.

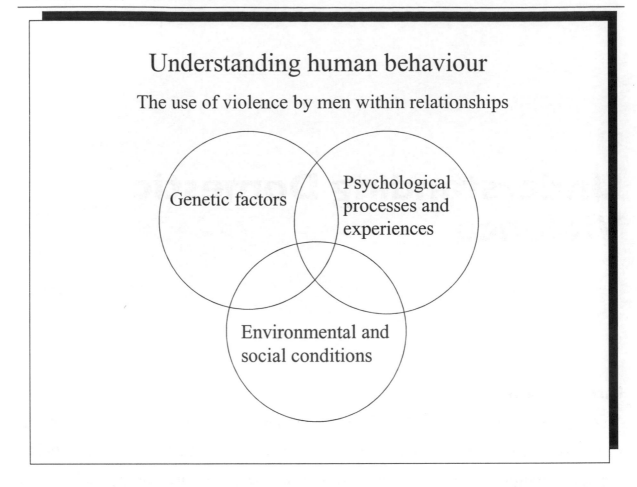

Figure 2.1. A model for understanding the use of violence by men within relationships (adapted from Covey 1992).

A male violence gene?

Research into human communities around the world is clear and consistent on one point: from tribal hunter groups to medieval societies to modern communities, the probability that a same-sex murder has been committed by a man not a woman varies between 85 and 100 per cent and is usually greater than 90 per cent (Wrangham and Peterson 1997). What is it about being male and its 'muscular, propulsive, hormone driven, often chaotic force' (Sheehy 1998, p.97) that makes the use of violence so prevalent? Is there a violent gene within the male bloodstream?

Recent and ongoing developments in the field of neuroscience have identified differences in the physical structure and chemistry of the brain between males and females. It has been suggested that because of higher activity levels, hormones, neurotransmitters, or some yet undiscovered biological force, it may take less stimulation to push the average male over the aggression threshold than it does the average female (Kilmartin 1994). As with much of the work within genetics, there is a limited amount of hard evidence. At this point, it is possible to draw only tentative conclusions with regard to the genetic or biological role when attempting to explain the differences in aggression between males and females.

There are two obvious factors that clearly put serious question marks against a simple genetic explanation of men's aggressive behaviour. First, there are a lot of men who do not use violent behaviour. Second, there is also growing evidence of the use of violent behaviour by women. For example, one study has identified a worrying trend of teenage girls joining gangs and increasingly using physical force to get what they want (Wilkinson and Mulgan 1995). Other research has identified significant levels of violence being used by women against their partners, although of a less extensive and serious nature than violence by men within relationships (Mirrlees-Black 1999).

Psychopathy

A more tangible influence of genetics has arisen from recent research into the cause of psychopathy. This has suggested a major gene locus and that there may be evidence of 'an inherited component to psychopathy or the closely related concepts of anti-social personality disorder and conduct disorder' (Rice 1997, p.419). One of the distinguishing features of psychopathy is the apparent inability of psychopaths to experience empathy with or compassion for the victims of their violence. One research project sought to explain such a situation. The research involved the delivery of electrical shocks to a group of men classified as psychopaths. Disregarding the ethical dilemmas of such an experiment, what emerged was evidence that the subjects showed no sign of a normal physiological fear response. They had no sense of fear in themselves or in others. This situation appeared to be related to physiological irregularities in the workings of part of the brain which may be related to genetic or biological make-up (Patrick 1994). The tentative conclusion is that some individuals may be genetically predetermined to be unable to be empathic and are thus capable of inflicting great suffering on others.

At the time of writing, efforts are under way in the British Parliament to introduce legislation to allow for the detention of people classified as psychopaths and dangerous, even before they have committed further acts of violence. This reflects the current view that there may be a small group of people for whom it is now possible to forecast with some accuracy the likelihood of further violent offending.

Caution is necessary in the area of genetics. Ambitious claims have been made for it in the past and have then been discredited. There is much controversy and disagreement. Nevertheless, research is continuing at a rapid rate and an open and critical mind is required to learn from the findings which may emerge.

Psychological Processes and Experiences

How do psychological processes feed into a man's subsequent use of violence against his partner? Are their links between childhood experiences and upbringing to the subsequent development of violent ways of behaving? Again, there is a significant and growing body of material which seeks to throw light on this relationship.

Early developmental problems

Proponents of classical psychoanalysis have argued that ultimately the roots of the violence may be found in a variety of psychological problems stemming from early experiences (Bowlby 1988). They have demonstrated how those who do not experience emotional security and soothing, loving relationships as young babies and children do not learn how to soothe themselves and to become the caretakers of their own emotions. A range of early developmental problems may give rise to a poor self-concept and emotional dependency, leading to over-reactions to real or imagined threats in a violent manner. These individuals may become vulnerable to the pressures of coping with emotional upheaval and stress in later life. For some this may mean an inability to cope with emotions such as anger, rage and jealousy without resorting to extreme aggression and violence. This 'insight' model is the traditional approach to understanding violence. Though it comes in many forms the basic premise is that certain intrapsychic-type problems give rise to violent behaviours.

As with genetic explanations, there are significant question marks against such an approach in explaining fully the range of men who become involved in violent behaviours. Many men who experience psychological problems do not become violent to their partners. More significantly, there is also much evidence that men who have been violent within relationships do not appear to be suffering from psychological problems. As one expert in the field found, they frequently fare well in psychological testing (Bancroft 1997).

Learning within the family

More relevant to understanding the roots of individual men's use of violence against their partners may be their experience of parental conflict and the aggressive behaviour they have witnessed as children. Research has shown these factors to be significant in the future use of violence by individuals (Farrington and West 1990). It is also the case that there appears to be a higher likelihood of wife-assault in a population of males who have observed their mothers being assaulted by their fathers than in those who have been subject to physical abuse themselves. This is reflected in one theory of aggression which views aggressive responses as being shaped through the individual's learning history (Bandura 1973). A young boy growing up in a family may observe his father using controlling and violent behaviours with his mother. He may learn that such behaviours get his father what he wants and that he in turn can use aggression to get what he wants. As he gets older the boy may also discover how his own use of this type of behaviour can reduce his stress and tension, helping him deal with uncomfortable situations and get agreement and compliance from those around him. Over time such behaviour may come to be seen by him as appropriate, intentional and functional. It may begin to take on a self-reinforcing aspect. There is significant evidence to show that aggressive children tend to become violent teenagers and adults (Gulbenkian Foundation 1995).

Again caution is required, as there does not appear to be an automatic negative impact from living in such situations. Children are resilient. It is important to remember that some children remain perfectly well adjusted despite living with abuse (Mullender and Morley 1994). There are examples of boys who experience violence as children and who see their mothers being subject to violence siding with their mothers and determining to distance themselves from the use of such violence (Corrigan 1999).

Fatherless families

Research is beginning to throw light on the negative effects on children of having no father available in their homes or in their lives. 'Boys with no fathers or with fathers who are not around much, are much more likely to be violent' (Biddulph 1994, p.133). In one 26-year longitudinal study of empathy, researchers found that the single factor most linked to empathic concern was the level of paternal involvement in child care (Miedzian 1992). If one accepts that violence is related to a failure of empathy, then the implications for future behaviour are clear.

It is important to stress that it is not so much that female parents are doing something wrong, but rather that boys (and girls for that matter) need positive, committed fathers in their lives. There are key tasks in helping boys move through childhood, adolescence and into adulthood which include active involvement, play, setting limits, managing aggression and anger, mentoring, protecting from violence and aggression, and involving other men as positive role models. One source has also highlighted the critical developmental task for boys of being able to separate emotionally from their mothers in order to achieve satisfying and appropriate intimate relationships with women later in their lives. This complex task is more likely to be achieved with a strong, positive and present father or other idealised male (Gillette 1992).

It needs to be asserted that single female parents can and do successfully rear male children. However, there is some evidence that the opting-out and disappearance from the family scene of men may be an important element in our understanding of the violence of some young men against their girlfriends and partners. (There may also be some connection here to the related problem of domestic violence by sons towards their mothers.)

Environmental and Social Conditions

Perhaps the intrafamilial and psychological processes identified above are really reflecting wider societal and environmental forces and pressures. How does the social context and conditioning relate to the use of controlling and abusive behaviours by men against their partners?

Masculinity

Some commentators have pointed to the socialisation processes that operate on young boys within our society as being relevant to their future violent behaviour. For example, many men go through a process which appears to encourage them to repress their feelings, to be competitive and aggressive, to be in charge and tough, and to take risks (Murphy 1996). A macho, masculine mystique is promoted. Some men present as 'stubborn, cocky, hard to read, convinced that they must remain forever strong, perpetually virile, providers and protectors of their families, and without doubts or needs or fears that require expressing their feelings' (Sheehy 1996, p.xvi). It is clear that the formation of such identities may well play out in terms of future involvement in aggressive and destructive behaviour aimed at other men, women and themselves.

What happens when negative elements such as social deprivation and exclusion from opportunities for education and a meaningful role within society are also present? As one commentator put it, then masculinity often asserts itself as a 'frightening, fearless fraternity of criminal, hard men' who often terrorise local communities and abandon young women (Campbell 1993, p.50). Many men enduring such damaging processes then expect and demand that their female partners take care of their emotional needs.

Violence within society

The situation in Northern Ireland also contains another volatile element related to ongoing divisions and political instability. For some men, violence has been seen as a legitimate means to resolve conflict and disagreement. How do young men who have been brought up within such a culture and set of experiences, who have been prepared to maim and kill, behave within relationships and families? Is there not a danger that they may also be more likely to use violence and intimidation to resolve conflict within the home?

Patriarchy and power and control

Northern Ireland is also a relatively conservative society where traditional beliefs value the family unit and in some ways tend to subordinate the woman's role within it. The feminist analysis of male violence against known partners seeks to place it within such historical, cultural and situational contexts. It emphasises the concept of patriarchy and the imbalance of power in male–female relationships as being central to explaining domestic violence (Dobash and Dobash 1992). From this perspective, male power has been built into relationships historically, through laws which assume that men have the right to authority over women and children. Domestic violence arises from men's efforts to exert or maintain such power or as a reaction to a perceived loss of such power. The strength of such an analysis is evidenced when one considers four significant sources of conflict which appear to lead to violent attacks by men on women. These are:

1. possessiveness and jealousy
2. men's expectations concerning women's domestic work
3. men's sense of right to punish their women for perceived wrongdoing
4. the importance to men of maintaining and exercising their positions of authority.

There is a clear intentional and purposeful aspect to the violence. Coupled with the concerns about young men's conditioning and behaviour raised earlier, the possibility of violence is always present. 'Individual attitudes endorsing male supremacy and the legitimacy of violence will be predictive of male violence' (Archer 1994, p.319).

The feminist analysis has also contributed to a broader understanding of what domestic violence actually is. Within such an understanding, it can be viewed as 'any act that causes the victim to do something she does not want to do, prevents her from doing something she wants to do, or causes her to be afraid' (Adams 1988, p.191). In other words it involves a continuum of 'unwanted, coercive, cruel and gendered behaviour' (Mullender 1996).

Clearly, issues of patriarchy and power and control are essential in understanding the nature of male violence against women. However, there are studies to show that not all men who hold sexist views use violent and controlling behaviours. There is also some research which suggests that abusive men do not hold significantly more traditional attitudes towards women than non-abusers (Hotaling and Sugarman 1986). Whilst the social context is obviously relevant, the difficulty remains that structural explanations do not on their own fully explain the decisions of particular individuals to exercise violence.

Conclusion

In this brief overview, I have sought to present a range of explanations, theories and research findings which seek to increase our understanding of the complex issue of why some men use violent and aggressive behaviours within their relationships. The three areas covered in this chapter artificially break up and compartmentalise the complex, messy reality of violent behaviour. There is a danger that an over-strict adherence to a particular theoretical approach or to an ideological view may limit a full understanding of a particular individual's behaviour. It is probably within the interaction of personal, background and social factors that a fuller understanding of the individual's behaviour can be found, and the various human and social sciences will continue to provide insights and information about such behaviour. Whilst much useful work has been carried out, our understanding of why particular individuals will use violence is still relatively limited. 'There is as yet no universally accepted agreement about why men use violence to women partners' (Morran and Wilson 1999, p.75). This is reflected in the fact that at the time of writing, the Economic and Social Research Council has commissioned a five-year Violence Research Programme (1997–2002). This has funded 20 separate research projects in England, Wales, Scotland and Northern Ireland to explore further violence to the person, including male violence within relationships. We are all still learning.

Behaviour is not predetermined

It is my view that it will not be possible to reach a situation in which we will be able to explain fully all aspects of human behaviour, including violence. Our behaviour, violent or otherwise, is not predictable. We are not determined by our genes or circumstances. 'The deterministic map gives a skewed picture of our own deep inner nature, and it denies our fundamental power to choose' (Covey 1999, p.349). A core belief which underpins this book is in the sense of uniqueness and mystery within each individual person. We have physical, mental, emotional and spiritual dimensions. As individuals we have the ability to stand apart from and become aware of our thinking, feelings and behaviours. Ultimately there is freedom of choice and the ability to change.

The way forward

The PVR programme seeks to combine this belief in change, and to relate it to the various themes that have emerged in this chapter. The men who are prone to the behaviours under question have been influenced by a combination of the personal, familial and social factors already identified. They have developed a belief system, a way of seeing the world, in which controlling and violent behaviour of some sort will be used and condoned as resolving or avoiding conflict (Russell 1995). It is this mindset, which has come out of their personal, familial and social experiences, that provides the understanding of the behaviour and that needs to be addressed. This aggressive and controlling mindset, however subtle, sophisticated, hidden or masked, and the behaviour that comes from it, are the primary issues. The PVR programme which is outlined in the second part of this book is provided as a means for those men who are motivated to do so to undertake the work of evaluating, addressing and confronting their own mindsets and resultant behaviours.

3

The Learning Process and Theory for Practice

Introduction

The previous chapter overviewed a range of explanations that have been put forward to explain the use of controlling and violent behaviour by some men within their relationships. Whilst awareness of some of these 'causes' is important in helping to explain this violence, the reality remains that there is only one person who is responsible for the use of violence. The fundamental starting-point of the programme is that the person who uses violence is responsible for it. It is imperative that participants are aware that it is their use of aggressive, abusive or violent behaviour that is the primary issue. This is not to deny that men may often have experienced difficulties and pain in their lives and have a range of problems. They should be advised of resources which may be relevant to them, such as counselling, Alcoholics Anonymous, or other support groups. This programme may indirectly help them in dealing with some of their problems but the main focus will be on the pain that they cause, not the pain that they may be in.

The Learning Process

The PVR programme seeks to encourage participants to focus on something they have avoided and which they need to face up to. To do this and though it may sound inappropriate, they need to move as far away as possible from their own history, their relationships and particularly their partners' behaviour. (This is very difficult for some men to do, and should be seen as a goal to be worked at throughout the programme.) They need to concentrate on themselves and their own thoughts, feelings and actions. An atmosphere needs to be created that allows participants to speak freely about the selfish, controlling and abusive behaviour they have used. They need the space to analyse and unpack these thoughts, and eventually to be able to work towards understanding the thinking or mindsets that underlie the behaviours. Ultimately, if there is to be a positive learning experience, participants need to take responsibility for what they do and begin to move towards some change.

The methods and processes used to encourage and facilitate participants on such a journey will be briefly outlined. A working knowledge-base will be provided, including reference to several texts. These may be referred to by those who wish to increase their knowledge and continue to develop their practice.

Motivation and the Process of Change

It is more likely that a programme aimed at helping individuals change their behaviour will be effective if they themselves see the need to change. This motivation to change may be internal, as when someone is genuinely coming to realise the problems he is causing by his behaviour and sincerely wants things to be better. On the other hand it may be external, as in the case of someone realising that they are about to lose their partner. Perhaps in many cases it is a mixture of both.

The PVR programme is built on an understanding of the critical relationship between internal motivation and the change process. It aims to engage and motivate participants positively so that they really want to work through a difficult process of change. To this end, insights from the motivational interviewing approach have been incorporated into the programme (Miller and Rollnick 1991). Although used more extensively in individual work with those who are resistant to change, this approach provides a value-base and way of working upon which the programme is based. The method stresses the importance of the worker's style in obtaining positive outcomes. The process is as important as the content. The approach avoids an authoritarian, confrontational style. It involves listening and acknowledging, though not colluding with, the validity of the individual's experiences and perspectives. The five principles below provide a useful touchstone to which facilitators may relate their practice. Whilst it is the participants' responsibility to move through the change process, it is the responsibility of the facilitator to provide an environment which reflects the following principles.

1. *Express empathy.* There is full acceptance of the participants as individuals worthy of respect. Skilful reflective listening is fundamental in seeking to understand the participants' feelings and perspectives. There is an awareness and an acknowledgement that ambivalence about change is normal and the process is difficult.

2. *Develop discrepancy.* Hard information is presented to participants; the full effects of violent and controlling behaviours on direct victims, on children, on others, on relationships, and the long-term consequences for the abusers are explored in depth. Facilitators need continuously to bring to the fore factors that increase tensions between the way participants are presenting things and the reality of the effects of what they are doing. Participants need to experience some degree of 'psychological squirm' in considering the discrepancy between how they see themselves as persons and the fact that they are also perpetrators of abusive behaviour. Gently feeding back information to participants, softly confronting and challenging the way they see things, can augment their motivation in moving forward into change. It is only the first-hand realisation of one's own problems which 'will generate focused insight and sufficient energy for change' (Woodcock and Frances 1992, p.3). The goal of the motivational approach is to have the participant almost talk himself into deciding to change the abusive behaviour.

3. *Avoid argumentation.* Facilitators need to have the ability to avoid arguments, whether they are about proving a point or forcing home an 'insight'. The approach is not about getting into arguments and showing participants that they are mistaken. Offensive tactics bring out defensive reactions. An indicator of straying off course is open conflict and strong disagreements within the group. The goal is to try to encourage participants into a process of reflection and self-challenge through open-ended questions and selective feedback.

4. *Roll with resistance.* Accept that resistance to any sort of change is normal. Try to roll with it, move round it, go on to something else. It is always possible to come back to an issue. The facilitator needs to be flexible and sensitive and to be comfortable with the fact that she or he won't always have the answer or solution. Have faith in the slow impact of the programme. Over time it may begin to overcome the significant levels of distortion or minimisation that may be there. At the end of the day it's the responsibility of each man to do the work.

5. *Support Self-efficacy*. Emphasise personal responsibility and choice in the ability of participants to make some positive change in their behaviour. This is a critical issue as participants' expectations of themselves have a great deal to do with their willingness to make an effort and to cope with difficulties and setbacks. They need to have a sense and a belief that they can make some progress (Bandura 1986).

Motivation and the stages of change

The PVR programme, remaining close to the above principles, aims to assist participants through the stages of change (Prochaska and Di Clemente 1984). Figure 3.1 shows the process of change through which participants must strive to move. This process, the difficulties, the possibility of lapses, etc., are covered with participants in Stage 1 of the course. Given that PVR is a voluntary educational course, it is likely to attract participants with a level of acceptance and acknowledgement that they have a problem with their use of abusive behaviour. Nevertheless, as men move through the course, they may begin to feel uncomfortable with some of the inputs. As their rationalisations, denials and minimisations begin to be challenged, the importance of them staying with the course and not going through the motions for a quick fix becomes apparent. It is also possible that if this programme becomes more widely available to agencies such as social services, then the profile of participants may be more resistant to the need for change. There is some evidence that within some criminal justice system programmes, where initial resistance and apathy may be strong, the use of motivational approaches can be helpful in encouraging some to begin to move into a process of change (Dobash *et al.* 1996). Despite this, it remains my view that it is unlikely that an educational programme will significantly impact on those men who do not feel that they have a problem, or whose motivation to do the programme is totally related to external factors (Rosenfeld 1992). In assessing a participant for any positive programme of change, denial is a strong indicator of unsuitability.

Adult Learning Theory

The PVR programme is educational. In order to enhance the commitment to change, a large amount of information is provided to participants over the 26 sessions. This includes material on the causes, nature, extent and consequences of male domestic violence within relationships. Framing the course as educational and not therapy promotes the idea that men can learn to change, that they are not faulty individuals

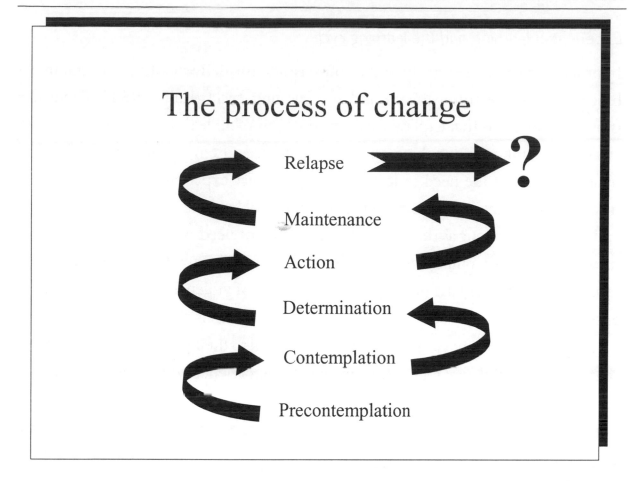

Figure 3.1. The process of change and PVR (adapted from Prochaska and Di Clemente 1984).

but rather men who have learned destructive messages about how to treat their partners. Whilst the programme is literacy-based, it seeks to offer a balanced approach which requires a mix of learning activities. These range from doing individual reading and written work and listening to presentations, to small and larger group discussions and more experiential exercises such as sculpts and playing out short scenarios. (See Appendix 2.)

Participants may come onto the programme with negative feelings about education and learning as a result of previous experiences. They may well have been through a system where they were told what to learn, had to learn by memory and learnt things that were not particularly relevant to them. They may have had negative experiences with teachers and trainers within a culture of limited support and encouragement and subsequently associate learning with failure. Their previous learning environments may have been very controlled, with mistakes being frowned on. In short, they may come to the programme with a range of blockages to potential learning and a lack of awareness of actually how to learn.

Experiential learning and the learning cycle

In order to respond positively to the above issues, the delivery of the programme is based on adult learning theory and the learning cycle (Kolb 1984). There is a growing consensus that experience forms the basis of all learning. Learning is about creating meanings and making sense of experience. Often we suppress or deny or treat as irrelevant the need to learn from a particular experience, and so we go no further. Participants are encouraged to see their problem with the use of controlling and violent behaviour as their learning experience or need. Within that general area they will identify numerous other learning needs during the programme. For example, why do they use only a particular amount of violence, how do they experience anger, what are the effects of their behaviour on their children, how have they played down their behaviour, how can they respond to their partner's anger in a more sensitive, respectful way, etc.? A learning need or experience will be lost or misunderstood unless it is critically reflected on in detail (Freire 1976). This reflection is vital but complex. It involves making a judgement on the experience, assessing and reassessing it in the light of other experiences and new information. A range of information is given through the programme both through direct inputs and through discussion and processing of participants' experiences. The importance of a growing knowledge-base within this process cannot be exaggerated. Without new knowledge there can be no critical reflection. Participants can then begin to observe themselves and their thoughts, feelings and behaviours, and to reflect at length on issues raised. Can they begin to recognise patterns and meanings from their experience?

The next stage of the learning process involves developing generalisations and coming to conclusions. With the new knowledge coming from the programme and their own personal work, they can begin to analyse their problem, make hypotheses and identify possible answers as to how it might be managed. (See Figure 3.2.)

The final stage in the learning cycle involves planning, preparing, setting goals and rehearsing behaviours. It is about beginning to test out different approaches and new ways of being within relationships. As a result, further learning needs may well arise and need to be addressed.

The above process is not automatic nor will it happen as neatly as outlined in these pages. It requires elements of goal-setting, making positive choices and taking hard decisions on the part of the participant which relate to the motivational issues dealt with earlier. It will be on the basis of firm goals and decisions that engagement with the positive learning process outlined may take place. The length of the programme

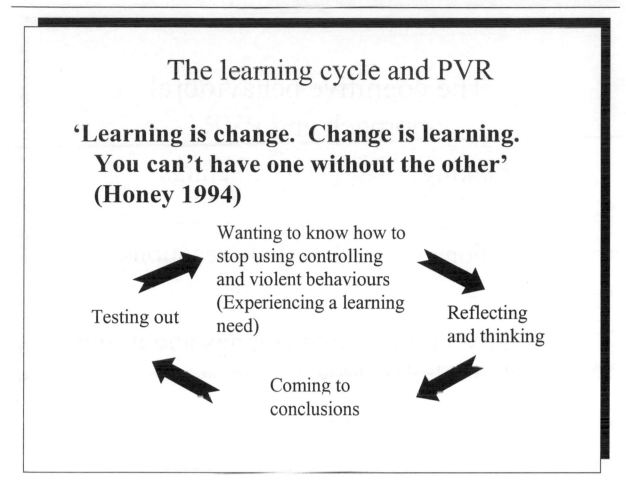

Figure 3.2. The learning cycle and PVR (adapted from Kolb 1984).

is deliberately set at 9–12 months to facilitate such a process, which involves a continuous cycle of experience, reflection, conceptualisation and testing out new learning. Work between sessions and check-ins are used in an effort to enhance the educational emphasis of the programme.

The Cognitive Behavioural Approach

The motivational and educational approaches are about the WHY of change. They are the base upon which the programme rests. The cognitive behavioural approach is about the HOW of change. It is the engine-room through which change occurs! Central to the PVR programme is the basic and simple truth that the way we see the world, the lens through which we look, the mindset we have, is a critical determinant in how we will actually behave (Covey 1992). The cognitive behavioural approach recognises the reality that significant aspects of our behaviour are influenced by subjective internal experiences, by thoughts, images, attitudes, beliefs, etc. (See Fig. 3.3.)

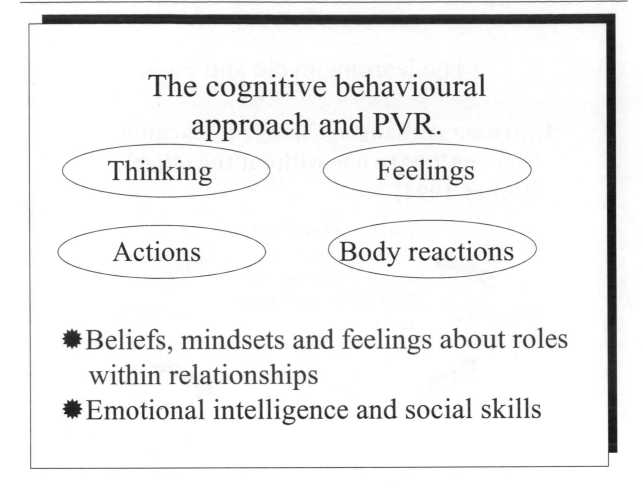

Figure 3.3. The cognitive behavioural approach and PVR.

The aim is to try to help participants increase their awareness of how particular cognitions are having a causal effect on their behaviour. It is about thinking, feeling and doing, about actual behaviour in the here and now. It focuses clearly on specific behaviours, the reasons behind them and the consequences they will have for the individual and for others.

Gender and power and control issues

The critical point is that the cognitive behavioural approach is used to focus on those ideas, beliefs and mindsets which specifically relate to the participant's use of controlling and abusive behaviours within relationships. At the heart of the PVR programme is a 'gender-based modality' (Gondolf 1997). This is a direct response to the important insights concerning patriarchy, power and control, masculinity, learning theory and sexist values referred to in the previous chapter. The critical area of thinking that requires attention is to do with those ideas and beliefs regarding social interaction between men and women which are embedded in society's fabric and which have been accepted without conscious awareness or examination by some men. Such beliefs have clear cognitive, affective and behavioural aspects. For example, the man who states that he deserves his wife's attention when he comes home from work is 'describing not only his thinking, but his emotional predisposition as well as his likely behaviour towards her' (Russell 1995, p.18). These are the sorts of issues that the cognitive behavioural approach will help participants address. As they explore the wide range of actual behaviours that comprise domestic violence they will, it is hoped, begin to relate such behaviours to the distorted and negative mindset from which they are operating. They will be required to concentrate on the effects of their behaviour, and how it impacts on their partners and children; they will also see how it is in many ways a tactic to help them deal with difficult situations. The insights gained from being able to step back and analyse their actions in terms of their controlling effects and impact – as opposed to stated intentions or a response to a difficult situation – can be significant. This may be the beginning of accepting some responsibility for the use of particular behaviours.

Social skills and emotional intelligence

As well as being clearly linked to power and control and gender issues the cognitive behavioural approach is also used to address a range of other areas. Primarily these are the management of emotions such as anger and jealousy, stress handling, conflict resolution skills, and assertiveness. To take the example of anger, information is given to participants on its nature and its consequences and how it may relate to an individual's controlling and violent behaviour. As with other social skills, participants may not have deficits in their ability to manage anger in other areas of their lives, and anger on its own will not give a full understanding of their abusive behaviour. There are frequent observations from research that many men are not angry when they are being violent to their partners (Morran and Wilson 1999). However, for some men, anger management may be a relevant part of the intervention. A man may need to learn to try to manage his anger better before he can begin to work on the types of thinking and mindsets referred to above which may be triggering his anger in the first place. Sometimes the learning of new behaviours on their own may help loosen mental rigidity and distortions and help in taking on board new thinking.

Group Work

Whilst the programme can be delivered individually, the learning experience may be enhanced for participants within a positive group setting. The group experience can provide additional support as well as challenge. The awareness that other men are behaving similarly can provide participants with hope and can stimulate them into moving forward positively (see Fig. 3.4). Given the educational nature of the PVR programme, the group experience is structured and within contractually agreed limits. It is not a free-flowing, therapy-based experience. The approaches already outlined, along with the tightly structured curriculum of each session, ensure that group dynamics and interaction are not critical to the enterprise. However, once a group is formed, the processes of collective human action will begin to operate and it is helpful to work within the group in an informed and sensitive way. The *how* of group experience, the way in which a group discusses or acts together, will be reflected in the quality of group experience. It is not possible, nor is it necessary, to do justice to the vast array of material on group work theory and practice. Within the

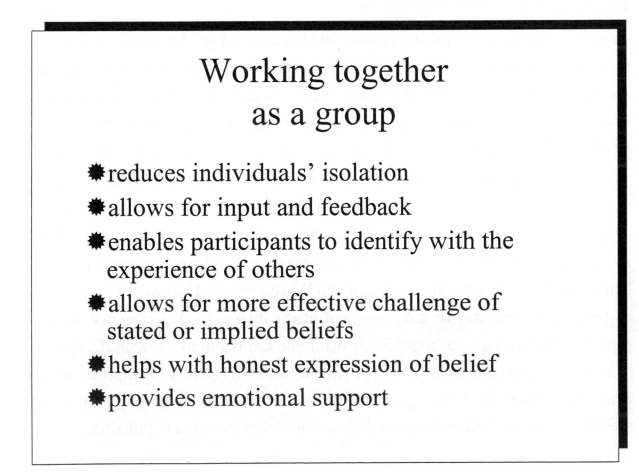

Working together as a group

* reduces individuals' isolation
* allows for input and feedback
* enables participants to identify with the experience of others
* allows for more effective challenge of stated or implied beliefs
* helps with honest expression of belief
* provides emotional support

Figure 3.4. Group work and PVR.

context of a preventative educational programme for motivated adults, the facilitator has two main roles.

Leading the group

Clearly and primarily the onus is on the facilitator to take responsibility for leading participants through the curriculum. It is important to claim this authority, otherwise there will be confusion, insecurity and suspicion within the group. This involves being competent and clear about the content and demonstrating commitment to the process. After reinforcing the group contract and agreeing working guidelines in the first session, the facilitator will need to stick to group tasks, pacing sessions appropriately, maintaining boundaries and avoiding unproductive and diversionary arguments. To achieve this the facilitator should seek to encourage a good overall level of participation, and in particular not allow one or two participants to dominate the sessions.

Communicating within the group

'Effective communication is a fundamental prerequisite for every aspect of group functioning' (Benson 1996, p.131). Recognising the group dynamics at work, the facilitator will need to communicate on two levels. First, as above, the facilitator will need to ensure that the content is covered and the group is kept to task, and second, and just as important, she or he will need to relate to each individual within the group. It is important to recognise the vulnerability of individual members and to seek to develop more positive intimate relationships that will assist in both maintaining the group and also in engaging participants in the challenging learning process. The facilitator will at times need to be able to respond, gently reflect back and encourage individuals to challenge a range of their own presenting behaviours which may include:

- displaying sexist attitudes or behaviours
- justifying their use of controlling abusive behaviour
- blaming the victim
- playing down the harm caused by their behaviour
- being threatening
- depersonalising their partner by not using her first name.

Ultimately, where a participant is not engaging positively and not complying with the programme contract, the responsibility will rest with the facilitator to work towards an ending and not allow negative involvement to disrupt the participation and progress of others.

Other Issues

Ethnicity

The programme seeks to be available to any man from whatever ethnic or religious background who acknowledges that he is causing difficulties by his behaviour within his relationship. The focus is clearly on behaviours that are generally agreed as causing distress and fear in women. The central issue is that whatever the cultural background, the use of behaviours which instil fear in women is not acceptable.

There is a need for sensitivity to and awareness of the cultural practices and expectations of members of different ethnic groupings, and to acknowledge their own experiences of racist and abusive behaviour. The programme needs to continue to strive to be accessible to such groupings.

Learning difficulties, including literacy problems

The programme is very much literacy-based and would prove difficult for those with limited skills in this area. Significant modification will be required to make it more accessible to such people. This is an important issue in terms of seeking to reach as wide a range of prospective participants as possible and will require further attention.

Co-working

Within the group work format there is a case for a co-working arrangement in terms of delivering the programme. A female and male facilitator can model positive and equal working relationships and can be a significant source of modelling and learning for participants. In addition, this may also be a useful way to assist in training people to deliver the programme. It may allow someone less experienced to work alongside a more experienced colleague and thereby build up their competence and confidence.

Resource issues may make it difficult to release two members of a team to run the programme. Given the educational and preventative nature of the course, it is possible for one facilitator to deliver it. I am unaware of any conclusive research on the respective benefits of co-working as opposed to using a single facilitator.

Conclusion

I have sought to overview the theoretical underpinning of the PVR programme in this chapter. The theory and models of practice appear precise, clear and obvious. Difficulties arise in weaving the preceding elements into actual practice. While this requires commitment and the continuing development of relevant interpersonal and communication skills on the part of the facilitator, it should not be viewed as an overwhelming and extremely daunting prospect. A background in social work is not an essential requirement to deliver such a course. Indeed, 'the reality of working with domestic violence is different from anything you would get on a social work course' (McWilliams and McKiernan 1993, p.67). There is nothing mysterious, mystical or earth-shattering in the material that has been outlined in this chapter and that is delivered in the programme. It is about working to get the balance right. The programme is more than common sense or practice wisdom; it involves striving towards research-minded and theory-based practice. This is accessible to anyone with the commitment to continue to develop and learn. 'Learning and applying theory to practice are both part of an active, cyclical process' (Thompson 1995, p.82). If you were to observe parts of the sessions, you would find that they are businesslike and focused. However, they are not dramatic or particularly dynamic, with insights regularly shattering participants' distorted thinking and conversion experiences erupting within the room! It can be a long, slow grind. It is the cumulative impact of the tightly designed programme and the participants' commitment and perseverance over many months that may eventually facilitate the beginnings of change.

4

Preventative Programmes and Risk Issues

Introduction

There are many behaviours that comprise male domestic violence. On one level are men who actually use very little or no *physical* violence. They may in fact view the use of such behaviour against a woman as being 'beneath them'. Nevertheless, such men may use a range of other behaviours which control and dominate and instil fear in their partners and families. The continuum ranges from such men, to those who use low-level occasional physical violence, to those who use more serious violence against their partners. They may or may not use similar behaviours in other areas of their lives. In addition, there are a small group of psychopathic, sadistic and extremely dangerous men. Given such a complex situation, both the civil and the criminal justice systems are used in seeking to respond to such behaviours.

Limitations of the Criminal Justice Response

The reality is that the formal justice system has gone only so far in tackling the problem. A small proportion of domestic violence actually ends up being dealt with in the criminal justice system. In Northern Ireland, it appears that (approximately) only 11 per cent of police cases actually proceed to prosecution (McWilliams and Spence 1996). A study in England indicated that even within an area which had a well-developed and co-ordinated domestic violence strategy, the prosecution rate remained disappointing (Kelly 1999). Other research has identified that less than one-third of female victims of domestic violence actually wanted arrest and legal intervention (Hoyle 1998). The reasons for this included: fear of retaliation, the desire not to break up relationships, and the view that the system was unhelpful. One commentator has stated that 'the criminal justice system as it stands is regarded by victims of domestic violence as an exceptionally clumsy and ineffective tool' (Hoyle 1998, p.205). The result is that a significant amount of violent behaviour is going on without perpetrators being held accountable.

The extent of the problem is regularly brought home to people in Northern Ireland when a man appears in court on his *first* domestic violence related offence and it relates to the murder of his wife or partner. It usually emerges in such cases that previous violence has taken place. Despite this, there has often been no previous contact with the legal system. Even in those cases where the man has been prosecuted, concerns have been raised as to whether the sentencing reflected the severity of the offending. 'Six months later the woman ends up dead' (McWilliams 1999).

Clearly, everything should be done to encourage victims to have their attackers held accountable for their violence. When serious assaults are downgraded, when prosecution is delayed, when women are not offered protection from further violence, then they may obviously conclude that the costs and risks of prosecution outweigh the consequences for their attackers (Hart 1993). The ongoing efforts to co-ordinate and strengthen the criminal justice response need to continue. These should include continuing improvements in investigatory and prosecution processes with relevant training for police, prosecutors, magistrates and judges. The emphasis should be on having the perpetrator held accountable for his criminal behaviour and on all efforts being made to effect a prosecution.

The situation is further exacerbated within the Northern Ireland context. Although the police have developed a range of positive and sensitive practices in this area, there are concerns that the communal and political conflict impedes effective policing for some women victims of domestic violence. Currently, the system is subject to a major review and there is real hope that structures and procedures can be found which will meet with the approval of the vast majority of people here. This may allow positive developments in this area to continue.

Given the issues raised above, it may be unwise to introduce criminal justice responses which seek to pressure or force women who have been subject to domestic violence to give evidence against their attacker. Whilst the intention may be to hold perpetrators accountable, the actual effect may actually be to disempower some women and further jeopardise their safety.

Developing Other Responses

More law enforcement will help. It sends out a clear message. However, at the same time it is not a panacea. In recognition of the complex nature of the issue there is also a need to develop a range of flexible and innovative approaches which seek to address the needs of victims and perpetrators alike.

Cautioning

A recent project in Leeds explored the use of a graded system that offers help to victims and also the perpetrators of violence against them. Within the project, men coming to the attention of the police for the first time were not automatically prosecuted but, with their partners' agreement, were cautioned. Not only did the victims feel that they had more control over how their situation was being handled, but it was also possible to focus on those more serious situations where further call-outs were required by the police (Hamner 1999). Such innovative schemes need to be encouraged and developed.

Educational strategies

Given the pervasive nature of domestic violence, there continues to be a need for a greater role for educational and preventative programmes. These should include work carried out with children at school or in youth clubs as well as with women who have been subject to such behaviours. There is also space for the type of educational programme outlined in this book. This will allow motivated men significantly to address their behaviour. These programmes may be offered in various ways:

- to any man who is beginning to recognise his need to change.

- within counselling situations for couples where both parties are indicating their desire to work at the relationship. An educational programme may ensure a man accepts and addresses his use of controlling behaviour. It will send out a clear signal that his behaviour is his responsibility. It is not something caused by the relationship. It should not be dealt with as part of the couple counselling process until he has seriously addressed his violence.

- linked to cautioning schemes or restorative justice projects to seek to reduce the chances of men moving further into criminal behaviour.

PVR, Prevention and Education

PVR has positioned itself on the preventative end of the continuum. On one level the first stage of the programme can be used as a general awareness-raising and information-giving course for men. The full programme is designed for those men who feel they have a problem with their use of violent and controlling behaviours. It is aimed at men who wish to address their behaviours in order to avoid committing serious criminal behaviour or causing serious harm to their partners and children. No prior assessment is carried out; all that is required is an acknowledgement that there is a problem with their behaviour in their relationship, a degree of motivation to work at it within an educational format and an agreement to comply with the programme contract (see Appendix 1). This includes a declaration that they are not currently facing any domestic violence charges.

PVR is not a criminal justice programme. It seeks through education and raising awareness to make a positive contribution to decreasing violence against women within our community. Of course, some participants may have already used behaviours which may be serious and should have been processed through the criminal justice system. A preventative approach in such cases may appear to conflict with the value of zero tolerance of domestic violence advocated in Chapter 1. Nevertheless, given that the prospect of a criminal conviction is not possible, is it not preferable to provide some means whereby the man can begin to address his unacceptable behaviour?

Educational and preventative intervention can never be a completely risk-free venture. Whilst it is unlikely that very dangerous men will have the desire to acknowledge that they have a problem and participate, caution is required. Practices and procedures need to be built in to acknowledge potential areas of risk.

Protecting Women

This is the key underpinning value upon which the PVR programme rests. The requirement that no physical violence occurs is emphasised and continually reinforced throughout the programme. Each participant is required to give details of his wife or partner, even if they are separated. She is contacted and information is given to her with regard to local Women's Aid services. In addition she is invited to attend a special information session two weeks after the programme has started (see p.56). In particular, partners are advised of the risk issues if they have already been experiencing significant physical violence. They need to be aware that there is significant evidence to suggest that men who are violent to their partners do not stop being violent, but often increase the frequency and severity of attacks. They also need to be told that there is limited evidence as yet as to the effectiveness of such programmes and it is vital, particularly if there has been a significant level of violence, that they keep in place a safety plan for themselves and their children (Mullender 1996). They should not be lulled into a false sense of hope. For example, it may happen that a man will refer himself so that he can return to his partner. It is important to advise the woman to base her decision on whether to reconstitute the relationship on a full safety assessment and not just on his statement of intent. He should be doing the programme with no strings attached!

In addition, if any disclosure or behaviour of a participant during the programme raises any concerns in relation to the risk and dangerousness issues explored below, then these will also be passed on to the participant's partner and she will be encouraged and supported in looking at her own safety.

Protecting Children

With regard to children there is no room for discretion. If there is information coming from any of the participants which indicates that children have been abused, the details should be passed on to the child protection agency. Research indicates that within violent, coercive family environments the probability of child physical abuse increases, as for that matter does child sexual abuse – both are a function of the misuse of personal power by the man (Goddard and Hiller 1993).

On a more general level there is the whole issue of children who are not being directly abused, but who nevertheless may be witnessing the abusive and controlling behaviour against their mothers. Statistics from the 1996 British crime survey showed that about one-third of victims said that their children had been aware of the last assault (Mirrlees-Black 1999). Concerns about the impact of such a situation on children remain ever-present. Courts in Northern Ireland are now required to address such issues when considering contact or residence orders between a child and someone who has been made subject to a non-molestation order. A key criterion is whether the child is at risk of harm as a result of seeing or hearing the ill-treatment of another person (Children (NI) Order 1995).

Impact on children is one of the central themes covered on the course. On a potentially positive note, it is fear about the effects on their children that is sometimes the main motivating force for some participants to do the programme. The programme does encourage men to take part in meaningful, necessary and challenging interactions on the whole issue of how their children are being affected. This may play out positively in some situations where there are concerns about children and may often be a source of powerful and positive learning and change for participants. It may also begin to address some of the issues around the avoidance of child protection issues with men which have been evident in some child protection work (O'Hagan 1997).

Safety of Facilitators

The PVR programme is an educational, preventative intervention for motivated adults who are attending on a voluntary basis. Having worked as a facilitator for approximately a year, I have yet to experience any concerns about my own safety. Nevertheless, there is always the potential that a man who is dangerous may become involved. Basic common-sense measures should be incorporated into the structure and delivery of the programme. These should include a public and protected location for the programme and personal details about the facilitators being kept confidential.

Partnership and Co-operation

It is important to align with and be answerable to organisations operating in this area. Primarily this has involved close communication with Women's Aid, and a range of relationship counselling and child protection groups (Relate, Accord, Barnardo's, Community Safety, etc.). Such alliances are necessary in working with risk issues. The representatives of the above agencies can make links to the partners at the information session. They can then seek to encourage them to avail themselves of services that may help in exploring issues to do with having been a victim of such behaviour. Forming positive alliances and working in partnership are important strategies in lessening the risk issues involved. Receiving supervision or consultation from agencies such as Women's Aid is strongly recommended. This may allow risk issues and the dangers of collusion to be regularly addressed.

Risk and Dangerousness

It is not possible to separate abusive men into groupings that can be compartmentalised into particular risk categories so that particular and specific interventions can be delivered to them. The murkiness of the reality needs to be accepted and risk issues acknowledged and addressed as fully as possible. It is vital to stress that in this area, as in others to do with human behaviour, risk assessment remains an inexact science. 'It cannot be emphasised too strongly that the multiplicity of potential risk factors, and their likely interaction makes it difficult to predict accurately which individuals will become violent' (Gulbenkian Foundation 1995). Indeed, the issue of dangerousness and lethality remains one of the most challenging facing practitioners and researchers (Hart 1994). Bearing this in mind, I have listed below some of the accepted critical factors.

Previous behaviour of perpetrator

It is widely acknowledged that past behaviour remains the best predictor of future behaviour. The critical point is that if violent behaviour has been used in the past, it is likely to be used again. Each time the perpetrator commits a serious act without significant consequences the possibility of repetition is increased. It is also likely that the abuse may increase in frequency and severity over time (Straus and Gelles 1990). Indeed, the frequency (two–three times per month) and severity (requiring hospitalisation of victim) of previous assaults are relevant indicators in predicting future lethal violence even if other items on this checklist are not pronounced (Campbell 1995). Perpetrators who have previously committed sexual violence against their partners are almost twice as likely to commit a dangerous or lethal act of violence against them than those who have not (Bancroft 1997).

It is also important to take note of the degree of threatening behaviour that the participant may have used. Threats should be viewed as statements of future intentions and not just as tactics to deal with a particular situation. Even in the absence of previous physical violence, persistent threats may be accurate indicators of future behaviour (Hart 1994).

Views, beliefs, behaviours and situation of victim

The insights of the victim of domestic violence – the level of fear she experiences and her concerns for her own safety – should be taken seriously. Many victims will underestimate the danger but it is quite rare for them to overestimate it. Even where other points from this checklist are missing, the victims' views are relevant in distinguishing those cases where serious, life-threatening violence may occur from the majority of cases which are characterised by episodic, relatively minor attacks. Women who have experienced violence and their advocates routinely make judgements about safety, many of which prove to be beneficial and life-saving (Hart 1994).

The victim is attempting to end the relationship

There is no time of greater danger for a victim of domestic violence than when she attempts to get away from the perpetrator. This is the time when the majority of killings take place.

Psychopathic, anti-social, and criminal tendencies of perpetrator

Research is beginning to identify a possible category of abuser characterised as having psychopathic (little empathy and no remorse) and anti-social tendencies (Gondolf 1997). One study has highlighted the cold, manipulating nature of such men. Their violence appears to be a calculated act of terrorism, a method of controlling their wives by instilling fear. Extreme behaviours may include killing pets, describing violent fantasies in gory detail, cutting out newspaper articles about killings and leaving them about the house, or holding their victim out of an upper storey window. Their violence is carried out in a cold, calculating state – as they become more belligerent and abusive they are actually growing physiologically calmer (Jacobson et al. 1994). Such men often have long criminal records resulting from a range of violent behaviours and often have been involved in conflictual relationships with authority figures; they can be very dangerous to their partners and others. One study has indicated that the partners of psychopathic and anti-social types were actually less likely to leave or get free from such men (Gottman et al. 1995).

Obsession and extreme jealousy of perpetrator

Caution is required in dealing with a man who demonstrates attitudes of ownership towards his wife or partner. Extreme jealousy and efforts to isolate the victim from all outside contact are key examples of this. The man may make irrational accusations and may have delusional jealousy and unfounded suspicions filling his mind. Such a man may monitor his partner's whereabouts and make threats against her if she leaves him. This type of person is more likely to stalk, kill or injure his partner, even months or years after she has left him (Hart 1994). He is the type of man who believes he has an absolute right to his wife and her loyalty no matter what.

Misogyny

Evidence of hatred of women by a male perpetrator has been linked to a propensity to commit a murder or other dangerous assaults against a woman. Watch out for evidence of violent or hateful statements that have been made against women as a group (Bancroft 1997).

Substance abuse

Alcohol and drugs do not themselves cause violence and abusive behaviour. However, they can play an instrumental role in accelerating and worsening the level of violence. Assaults have the potential to become more severe and damaging with little or no warning. It is also the case that an ongoing serious addiction problem will greatly impede any possible learning or the prospect of positive change.

Availability of weapons, including use of martial arts and similar training

The use of weapons or martial arts in violent incidents usually indicates an increased risk of serious harm. Verbal reference to a weapon should also be considered. In other words, if the man has said: 'I should use my gun, that will sort you out', this should be considered as similar to the gun having been taken out and pointed! The wide availability of weapons in Northern Ireland is an area of concern and should be addressed.

Mental illness

There is some evidence that a man who uses violence against his partner and who then becomes acutely depressed or paranoid may be a candidate for homicide or suicide. Research shows that many men who are hospitalised for depression have homicidal fantasies directed at family members (Hart 1994). The risks from such mental illness will be greatly increased if there are ongoing problems with drugs or alcohol. (The vast majority of perpetrators do not have significant mental health problems.)

Conclusion

It is unlikely that any participant in a preventative educational programme for men who are acknowledging that they need to address their behaviour and are motivated to do so, will obviously be in the high risk and dangerous categories identified in this chapter. However, it is not possible to guarantee that all participants will be positively motivated and seriously open to making changes in their behaviours. Some participants may be reacting to external factors such as losing their partner or losing contact with their children; they may seek to pursue the course for such reasons and may even do so in a manipulative or negative way. It is imperative to remember that we do not have diagnostic, explanatory or predictive categories which allow us with any certainty to identify those men who pose the most danger to their partners.

Ongoing vigilance and caution are required. The desire to be positive, to succeed with participants, may lead one to be too optimistic about situations and lower one's guard. The safety of women and the duty to warn are the bottom lines. It is critical to have the ability to respond appropriately to new information that may be gained from participants' behaviours or disclosures within sessions, or from their partners. Risk factors may vary from week to week as circumstances change. The importance of procedures and partnership, of being clear about the value-base, of having some awareness of what research and experience tells us about risk, will help. As well as these, and just as important, may be the facilitator's intuition and gut feeling reached in consultation with the partner and other agencies. This instinct should never be undervalued as a guide in assessing dangerousness.

PART II

The Preventing Violence in Relationships Programme

The Preventing Violence in Relationships Programme

The PVR programme comprises 26 sessions, running over a period of approximately 9–12 months. There are three stages; the first two stages involve 20 weekly sessions in total. Stage 3 is made up of six sessions spread over a period of at least three months. (If required, an optional information session can be provided before the programme commences. This is contained in Appendix 1.)

(Each group session should take approximately 1½–2 hours.)

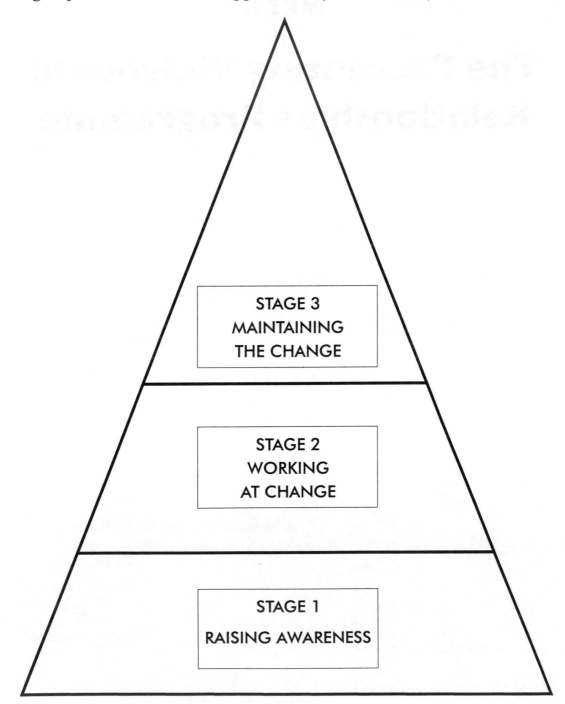

STAGE 3
MAINTAINING
THE CHANGE

STAGE 2
WORKING
AT CHANGE

STAGE 1
RAISING AWARENESS

5

Stage 1: Raising Awareness

This is the base upon which the programme rests. It involves eight awareness-raising sessions which address central issues. It is intended that by the end of the eight weeks, participants will have increased their understanding and awareness of the following areas:

- the definition and extent of domestic violence
- the degree to which they use abusive behaviours
- the impact of domestic violence on victims and children
- masculinity and power and control issues within relationships
- managing difficult feelings and emotional intelligence
- relevant distorted-thinking processes
- the process of change
- society's changing response to domestic violence.

As indicated earlier, this section of the course can stand on its own as an awareness-raising programme for men in general. It will allow any man to look closely at the subject-matter in a safe, non-threatening way. It will facilitate a self-examination and assessment of one's behaviour as well as providing detailed information and ideas on the subject.

Participants who have a real need to address their use of controlling behaviours within their relationships should leave Stage 1 feeling fairly shaken up. They should be able to make some connection between the programme content and their own particular situation and prepare to move into the difficult process of change.

Partners' Information Session

Two weeks after the commencement of the programme, wives or partners are invited to a separate information session. This session is an informal opportunity for partners to get information on the programme and to raise any questions or issues. It will also be possible to give them information about the range of services available to them. Representatives from Belfast Women's Aid, Relate and Barnardo's have attended this meeting of the Belfast PVR programme. It is crucial to have a partnership with agencies and organisations which offer services to women and are knowledgeable about victim issues in the area of domestic violence (see pp.46–47).

Stage 1 Session 1

Objectives of session

Participants will:

1. become aware of programme format and style

2. begin to understand the wide range of behaviours that are involved in domestic violence

3. become more aware of the purposeful nature of domestic violence.

Outline of session

Content	Methods and process
1. Welcome, introduction and outlining of objectives	Affirming and positive. (See facilitator's guidelines, p.59) Each participant to introduce themselves by their first name and also to give at least one reason why they have started the programme.
2. Setting the context, aims and objectives of PVR	Briefly outline the extent and seriousness of domestic violence and the objectives of PVR. (See pp.60–61)
3. Re-contracting	Briefly revisit. Allow for clarification and stress importance of child protection issues and also of not using the programme to seek to avoid being held accountable for offending behaviour.
4. Agreeing group guidelines. Identifying helpful ways of working together as a group	Brainstorm and agree with participants guidelines and ways of relating to each other that will encourage positive participation in the course. (See suggested guidelines p.62) Ensure that participants accept that if they have to refer to their wives or partners that they use their first names and try not to depersonalise them as 'she' or 'her' all the time.
5. Defining domestic violence	Work in small groups. Each group has five minutes to agree a definition of what domestic violence is, using no more than 20 words.

Stage 1 Session 1 (continued)

Content	Methods and process
5. Defining domestic violence (continued)	Process in larger group. Ensure that violence is not viewed in a narrow way, focusing just on serious physical violence. Work to ensure that a broad definition is agreed which includes physical, psychological, verbal, emotional, sexual and economic behaviours. Emphasise that the various behaviours are used to exert control. Share PVR working definition. (see p.63)

6. Exploring the use of violence within a relationship	View video of man using violent behaviour against his partner. Put following questions on flip chart and ask participants to work through them. (If video not available use attached script, p.65)
	
	 What abusive actions did the man use to exert control?
	 What were the man's intentions?
	 What beliefs do you think the man has about relationships and his role?
	 What were the effects of his behaviour on:
	
	     1. himself
	     2. his partner
	     3. the children?
	
	 What would the impact of previous violence be on this situation?
	
	 Highlight the intentional nature of the behaviour and the fact that things don't just happen. Don't spend too long on this exercise: it is intended to throw up a range of important issues which the course will be focusing on in depth.

7. Facing the challenge	Write up on flip chart: '**To complete this programme and change my behaviour**'. Ask participants to reflect individually on this for a few moments and note down the following. (1) how they actually feel about it, (2) what will help them achieve the challenge and (3) what will hinder them. Process briefly within group by taking main feelings (one positive and one negative), one source of help and one hindrance from each man.
8. Working between sessions	See exercise below.
9. Unwinding and closure	See guidelines, p.126.

Facilitator's guidelines on beginning a new programme

It is important to begin the programme positively: it is about trying to build on participants' courage and commitment in embarking on a difficult journey of change. At the same time, it is critical to put down a marker at this early stage that the programme is about challenging and not colluding with participants' negative attitudes and behaviours. The following points should be made:

- Acknowledge each participant's courage in being prepared to state that they have a problem with their controlling and abusive behaviours.

- Emphasise that they have a unique opportunity, which men don't often have, to step back, talk about, think about and reflect on their behaviours.

- Point out that change is difficult. It is a process. There are no quick fixes or short cuts. It has to be worked at. You reap what you sow.

- Stress that participants may experience feelings of confusion, embarrassment and distress. They are here to have themselves challenged. It's not about helping them feel better about themselves. Such feelings may in fact be a good sign, that 'you're shaking yourself up'.

- Emphasise that it is an educational course based on adult learning principles. Participants will be treated with respect and as adults. Information will be provided, and they will be challenged to think about a wide range of issues. It will require commitment, determination, concentration and dedication. The responsibility to do the work rests with them.

- Finally, everyone is different. Each participant has his own unique history and experiences. The course is designed to cover as full a range of relevant issues as possible but some bits may be more relevant than others. Try to stay with it. There are common themes that run through much of the course and learning may come at you from somewhere you don't expect if you stay alert and involved.

Extent of Domestic Violence in NI

✸ Local and international surveys constantly highlight domestic violence as a major concern for women

✸ In 1998 there were **14429** reported incidents of domestic violence in NI of which :

- 6385 physical violence
- 90% victims women
- 3223 assaults
- 670 serious assaults
- 60 very serious assaults
- 21 rapes
- 10 murders

Figure 5.1. Stage 1 Session 1. Extent of domestic violence in Northern Ireland (Dept of Economic Development 1999).

Objectives of PVR Programme

To help participants:

* increase understanding of their use of controlling and abusive behaviour

* increase understanding of the effects of this behaviour

* take full responsibility for use of this behaviour

* change their behaviour so that they do not use violence against women and children

Figure 5.2. Stage 1 Session 1. Objectives of PVR programme.

Suggested guidelines for the group

- No put-downs

- Each person to speak for themselves

- Honesty

- Participate fully

- Confidentiality

- Right to pass

- Agree to disagree

- Respect for each other's views and opinions

- Don't talk too long

(It is vital that the guidelines do not conflict with the contract that all participants have signed on joining the programme, particularly in the area of ensuring that confidential or personal information about partners is not shared.)

Seek to allow the group to participate as much as possible in reaching agreement on the above points. You may have to make some suggestions to get things moving. It is the first session, so participants may well be new to this type of situation and slow about contributing.

Remember: no involvement, then no commitment.

What is domestic violence ?

'Domestic violence is the use of physical or emotional force or threat within close adult relationships in a way that causes harm or distress to victims. In addition to actual or threatened physical or sexual assault and damage to property, domestic violence includes non-physical intimidation, such as persistent verbal abuse, emotional blackmail and enforced social or financial deprivation'

Tackling Domestic Violence, A Policy for NI (DHSS and NIO) 1995

Figure 5.3. Stage 1 Session 1. What is domestic violence?

Working between sessions

Identify at least five things that the man could have done to avoid using violent and controlling behaviour:

1.

2.

3.

4.

5.

An example of domestic violence

He arrived home from work late. He had phoned during the day and there had been no answer. He found the lipstick on the hall table. She said 'hello' as he came into the kitchen. Their two children were up in bed.

'Where the hell were you today when I phoned?' he shouted before she could get out a friendly welcome to him. He stormed over to her and stood above her. He began shouting at her about her being out of the house. He didn't believe that she was at her mother's. He questioned her about the use of her make-up and lipstick, demanding that his dinner be ready for him and throwing it on the floor when she gave it to him out of the oven. He became more and more aggressive. When one of his young children, who had heard the racket, came down the stairs, he yelled at her to get back up to bed before he gave her a hiding. At this his wife became angry and threw herself between him and the door out of the kitchen up to the children.

She yelled back at him, asking him what sort of man he was to frighten little children like that.

He grabbed her by the shoulders, squeezing them hard and pushed her back against the door.

'What kind of man am I? What kind of man am I? I'll show you what kind of man,' he yelled…

Stage 1 Session 2

Objectives of session

Participants will:

1.   identify the abusive and controlling behaviours that they use

2.   learn the time-out and WASP coping strategies

3.   begin to identify their early warning signs.

Outline of session

Content	Methods and process
1. Welcome and outlining of objectives	
2. Processing work done since last session	Take one example from each participant. Record on flip chart and keep in view.
3. Assessing the extent of each participant's abusive behaviour	Each participant to work individually through self-assessment form (pp.68–72). Stress critical importance of trying to be as open and honest as possible about what they have done.
	Not looking for explanations or rationalisations, just put down on paper the ways that they have actually behaved.
	Participants are not required to disclose the behaviours they have used. Encourage each participant to share his immediate reactions to the questionnaire in group. Take time to process main feelings experienced by participants as a result of the exercise.
	Stress it's not about who's the worst or 'league tables'. However, it is important that each participant has an awareness of the exact behaviours he needs to address.
4. Time-out coping strategy	Introduce this by stressing that no other issue can be dealt with until non-violence and safety become the bottom line. Emphasise the responsibility on each man to find a way, under the worst conditions, when he is most upset, *not* to be physically harmful.

Stage 1 Session 2 (continued)

Content	Methods and process
4. Time-out coping strategy (continued)	Once they cross that line it is a slippery slope downwards.
	There is a proven method to help them ensure that they do not use violence against their partners, but it will work only if they are motivated and willing to use it.
	Time-out allows them to cool off physiologically by waiting out the adrenalin surge.
	Present attached model to participants, p.73.
	Discuss ways that this strategy may be abused, e.g. to avoid arguments, partner's anger, to get out of the house, etc.
	It is likely that participants may have used such an approach. Check whether they have done so in an agreed and positive way and also as a final resort when physical violence was imminent.
5. Thinking about early warning signs	Participants to break into small groups and list as many early warning signs as possible. Process within group. Assist participants to begin to see the different types of cues that each of them may have before becoming violent:
	• Situational location, time of day, car, etc.
	• Thinking negative thoughts: 'she's doing this on purpose', expectations
	• Feelings inadequate, angry, jealous flooding with emotions, etc.
	• Physiological eye movement, clenching fists, voice, head going fuzzy, etc.
6. WASP exercise	See exercise p.74.
7. Working between sessions	See below.
8. Unwinding and closure	See guidelines, p.126.

Assessing my controlling and abusive behaviours

Human behaviour cannot be neatly analysed and predicted. However, greater understanding and awareness of what you are actually doing may help you to identify things that you need to address, work at and try to change. Things can get worse if you don't deal with them.

Consider the six areas of controlling and abusive behaviours outlined below and, as openly and honestly as you can, identify the range of behaviours that you have used.

1. Using physical violence

Do you ever do any of the following to your wife or partner?

	NEVER	RARELY	SOMETIMES	OFTEN
Slap her?	☐	☐	☐	☐
Push or shove her?	☐	☐	☐	☐
Punch her in the face?	☐	☐	☐	☐
Punch her on the body, arms or legs?	☐	☐	☐	☐
Choke her?	☐	☐	☐	☐
Kick her?	☐	☐	☐	☐
Pull or drag her by the hair?	☐	☐	☐	☐
Twist her arm?	☐	☐	☐	☐
Hurt her when she is pregnant?	☐	☐	☐	☐
Hit her with objects?	☐	☐	☐	☐
Use a weapon against her?	☐	☐	☐	☐
Keep her awake?	☐	☐	☐	☐
Bite her?	☐	☐	☐	☐
Try to strangle, smother or drown her?	☐	☐	☐	☐
Use any other physical violence on her?	☐	☐	☐	☐

2. Using threats and intimidation

Do you ever do any of the following to your wife or partner?

	NEVER	RARELY	SOMETIMES	OFTEN
Shout and scream at her?	☐	☐	☐	☐
Swear at her?	☐	☐	☐	☐
Make angry gestures at her?	☐	☐	☐	☐
Stand over her?	☐	☐	☐	☐
Frighten her by a particular look or stare?	☐	☐	☐	☐
Get 'in her face'?	☐	☐	☐	☐
Point at her?	☐	☐	☐	☐
Make threats to hurt or kill her?	☐	☐	☐	☐
Stop her from moving or leaving a room?	☐	☐	☐	☐
Force her to do something against her will?	☐	☐	☐	☐
Threaten to throw her out of the house?	☐	☐	☐	☐
Throw things at her or about the room?	☐	☐	☐	☐
Damage her possessions or property	☐	☐	☐	☐
Lock her in or out of the house?	☐	☐	☐	☐
Stop her going to the police or make her drop charges?	☐	☐	☐	☐
Drive the car recklessly to frighten her?	☐	☐	☐	☐
Let on to strike but don't?	☐	☐	☐	☐
Threaten your children	☐	☐	☐	☐
Use other threatening behaviour?	☐	☐	☐	☐

3. Using sexually abusive behaviour

Do you ever do any of the following to your wife or partner?

	NEVER	RARELY	SOMETIMES	OFTEN
Pressurise her into having sex?	☐	☐	☐	☐
Call her useless in bed?	☐	☐	☐	☐
Pressurise her into looking at pornography?	☐	☐	☐	☐
Commit violent sexual acts against her?	☐	☐	☐	☐
Make fun of or ridicule parts of her body?	☐	☐	☐	☐
Put her at risk of having sexually transmitted diseases?	☐	☐	☐	☐
Tear off her clothes?	☐	☐	☐	☐
Have affairs?	☐	☐	☐	☐
Use other sexually abusive behaviour?	☐	☐	☐	☐

4. Using male privilege and economic control

Have you ever done any of the following to your wife or partner?

	NEVER	RARELY	SOMETIMES	OFTEN
Withhold information about family income?	☐	☐	☐	☐
Keep cheque/banker's card from her?	☐	☐	☐	☐
Give her an allowance to manage on?	☐	☐	☐	☐
Expect her to pay for everything?	☐	☐	☐	☐
Control or limit the TV?	☐	☐	☐	☐
Make major decisions without her opinion?	☐	☐	☐	☐

4. Using male privilege and economic control (continued)

Have you ever done any of the following to your wife or partner?

	NEVER	RARELY	SOMETIMES	OFTEN
Boss her around and tell her the rules?	☐	☐	☐	☐
Decide what she wears?	☐	☐	☐	☐
Feel that you know better?	☐	☐	☐	☐
Decide both your roles within your relationship?	☐	☐	☐	☐
Refuse to care for the children?	☐	☐	☐	☐
Use any other controlling behaviours?	☐	☐	☐	☐

5. Isolating and not supporting

Do you ever do any of the following to your wife or partner?

	NEVER	RARELY	SOMETIMES	OFTEN
Stop her from seeing family or friends?	☐	☐	☐	☐
Limit her social life?	☐	☐	☐	☐
Stop or make it difficult for her to work?	☐	☐	☐	☐
Tell her that no one would give her a job?	☐	☐	☐	☐
Not let her drive the car?	☐	☐	☐	☐
Humiliate her in front of others?	☐	☐	☐	☐
Discourage her from going to places or seeing others?	☐	☐	☐	☐
Check up on her phone calls?	☐	☐	☐	☐
Criticise her family or friends?	☐	☐	☐	☐
Question her about her activities?	☐	☐	☐	☐

6. Using emotionally and verbally abusive behaviour

Do you ever do any of the following to your wife or partner?

	NEVER	RARELY	SOMETIMES	OFTEN
Tell her she is stupid, lazy, ugly, a terrible wife or mother, etc.	☐	☐	☐	☐
Tell her that no one else could ever love her?	☐	☐	☐	☐
Criticise her?	☐	☐	☐	☐
Criticise her family?	☐	☐	☐	☐
Not listen to her?	☐	☐	☐	☐
Constantly interrupt her?	☐	☐	☐	☐
Try to provoke an argument?	☐	☐	☐	☐
Twist her words?	☐	☐	☐	☐
Don't respect her feelings?	☐	☐	☐	☐
Blame her for your violence?	☐	☐	☐	☐
Play down or deny what you have done?	☐	☐	☐	☐
Have dramatic mood swings?	☐	☐	☐	☐
Try to make her feel guilty?	☐	☐	☐	☐
Threaten to harm or kill yourself?	☐	☐	☐	☐
Manipulate the children against her?	☐	☐	☐	☐
Behave in a very possessive or jealous way?	☐	☐	☐	☐
Use other emotionally abusive behaviour?	☐	☐	☐	☐

Time-out

It is your responsibility, even under the worst conditions, when you are most upset, not to be abusive and physically harmful to your partner.

A 'time-out' is a practical and proven tool you can use to prevent you doing or saying abusive things which you know you will regret later. A 'time-out' is a plan of action for removing yourself from your partner, or from any situation which you can see building up. It is an important way for you to show others, and yourself, that you can be in control of your behaviour and that you are capable of taking responsibility for yourself.

To plan your 'time-out' you need to go through the following series of steps:

1. Begin to become more aware of your early warning signs. They tell you that you are likely to be abusive if you don't remove yourself.

2. Explain what a 'time-out' is, to your partner. It is about making yourself safe and taking responsibility for your actions.

3. Agree with her what you will say or do so that your partner knows that you are not just walking out on her. This can simply be: 'I feel I need to take a 'time-out'.

4. Agree with her in advance how long your 'time-out' will last. (It is recommended that this should be at least one hour – you may find you want to make it longer.) A 'time-out' is a way of taking responsibility for your actions. If you say that it will last an hour, and you return one hour later, you will demonstrate that you are being responsible.

5. Plan what to do for your 'time-out'. It must involve you leaving the house. Just going to a different room means that you are too close.

6. The don'ts:

   Don't use 'time-out' unnecessarily – just to avoid an argument or to get out of the house.

   Don't drink – you need a clear head during that 'time-out'; alcohol will only make it worse.

   Don't drive – you are dangerous if you drive when your mind needs to be free to think.

   Don't go over and over the issue in your head.

The WASP: a guided imagery exercise

Ask participants to take a moment to relax in their seats. Suggest that it will help if they would close their eyes. Can they focus on their breathing – nice and calm and steady. Breathe deeply. Can they think back to childhood… Try to remember summer days and catching bees and wasps in a jar. Think about how different wasps reacted. Some settled onto the clover leaves and started resting or feeding. Others started flying about and buzzing and bashing into the side of the jam jar, their fear spilling over into frustration and anger and rage. It was almost like the wasps were shouting: 'I don't deserve this.' One wasp got more and more worked up but really only succeeded in making the situation worse.

Tell the men to try to hold that image of the righteous angry wasp for a moment and then ask them to come back into the present. Breathe evenly and open eyes when ready.

Ask participants if they have ever felt a bit like the wasp when they have been in interactions with their wives or partners. Get their descriptions of how they felt.

Then on the flip chart, use WASP to explain one tactic for helping them deal with such difficult interactions:

W = WAIT   Take time to see what is happening; don't just react.

A = ASSESS   What is it I want? What is important here? What could be the outcome if I react hastily? Am I afraid of something?

S = SLOWLY   Can I calmly work on the situation?

P = PROCEED   Should I take a time-out? How can I solve this problem?

(Waring and Wilson 1990)

Working between sessions

Think carefully about the six areas of controlling abusive behaviours that we explored in Session 2. Try to identify which of the main tactics you tend to use and write them down. These are the behaviours that you need to work at.

- **USING PHYSICAL VIOLENCE**

- **USING THREATS AND INTIMIDATION**

- **USING SEXUALLY ABUSIVE BEHAVIOUR**

- **USING MALE PRIVILEGE AND ECONOMIC CONTROL**

- **ISOLATING AND NOT SUPPORTING**

- **USING VERBALLY AND EMOTIONALLY ABUSIVE BEHAVIOUR**

Stage 1 Session 3

Objectives of session

Participants will:

1. increase awareness of the effects of domestic violence on women

2. increase awareness of the effects of domestic violence on children

3. learn an emergency coping strategy.

Outline of session

Content	Methods and process
1. Welcome and outlining of objectives	
2. Processing work done since last session	Each participant to identify the areas of his behaviour which seem to be the most controlling and abusive and which he needs to work at.
3. Effects of violence on women	Explain that the purpose of this exercise is to identify and recognise the short-term and long-term effects of domestic violence on women. Unless one begins to understand and appreciate the effects of such behaviour it is very easy to misunderstand victims' behaviour.
	Begin by briefly asking each participant to reflect on their own experience of ever being subjected to violent or abusive behaviour (*not* within their relationships). List key effects on flip chart.
	Then brainstorm on flip chart the various ways that women are affected by violence by their partners.
	Keep focus on the *effects* of violence on victims.
	Compare and contrast lists.
	(See guidance notes, p.78)
	Ensure discussion of important issues:
	• fear or fighting back – how can their partner's anger come out if they are afraid?
	• mixed feelings – confusion and anger, love and hate, etc.
	• effects likely to be long term
	• possibility that 'unreasonable' behaviour by partners may be a response to violence.

Stage 1 Session 3 (continued)

Content	Methods and process
3. Effects of violence on women (continued)	Finish exercise by having each participant identify at least two ways in which his own behaviour has affected his wife or partner.
4. Effects of violence on children	Introduce exercise by saying that everyone will now discuss how children of different ages are affected by domestic violence. Divide participants into five small groups. Set each group the task of answering the following two questions in about 10–15 minutes: • How would a child be exposed to or get drawn into violence within the family? • In what ways would the child be affected by the violence? Each group to answer the questions in respect of one of the following age ranges: Womb–1 / 2–4 / 5–12 / teen girl / teen boy. Reconvene, transfer each group's feedback onto flip chart and process. **Key points:** Effects can be severe and long-lasting. Also some 'effects' may be the methods that children use to survive and protect themselves in homes where there is violence. Children should not be labelled as 'bad' because they are displaying disturbed and difficult behaviours. Acting out behaviour is not abuse – it may be a response to abuse. Some participants may be shocked/upset at the extent of the harm they may have caused their children. You need to allow them to process their feelings. Focus on what they can do to begin to address the situation. It is never too late to take positive action. (Give men the handout on p.79.)
5. Emergency relaxation method	See p.80.
6. Working between sessions	See p.81.
7. Unwinding and closure	See guidelines, p.126.

Facilitator's guidelines on the effects of violence on women

Try to ensure that most of the following issues come out and are discussed.

FEAR	ANGER	PAIN

(Explore what it is like to be fearful and angry with someone at the same time. How do you get at them?)

Physical injuries — bruising – cuts – fractures – multiple injuries – death (develop in more detail)

Psychological impact — loss of self-respect and self-confidence – self-blame, suicidal feelings – humiliation – insecurity – shame – depression – distrust – resentment – hate – spite – revenge
loss of sexual feelings
confusion – ambivalence – mixed feelings

Behavioural consequences — loss of respect for you/doesn't feel like doing nice things for you
loss of sexual feelings for you
anger, sarcasm, apathy
passive resistance
not confiding/keeping secrets
alcohol, drug abuse and self-destructive behaviours
social isolation from family and friends
loss of money/income

The greater the uncertainty about the outcome the more terrifying the encounter

(Adapted from Goodman and Fallon 1995)

Domestic violence and children and young people

Ways that children will be drawn into violence against their mother	Effects of domestic violence on children and young people
Seeing it	Physical injuries, death
	Unsettled, tantrums
Hearing it	Fright
	Traumatised
Woken up from their sleep	Sleep disturbances, not eating well, sick, colicky baby
Harmed in the womb	Nervous, jumpy, crying a lot
	Not responsive
Ripped out of mother's arms	Speech difficulties
	Talking about it, acting out the behaviour
Toys broken	Withdrawn
	Problems with other children at nursery, school
Hit by mistake	Bed-wetting
	Fear, depression
Trying to stop it	Insecurity, low self-esteem
	School problems, or over-achiever
Hitting one parent	Develop problems to divert parents
	Prone to violence
Becoming abused themselves	Embarrassed by family
	Sexualised behaviour
Physically intervening	Getting into relationships too early
	Using alcohol and drugs
Telling someone	Confusion
	Self-harm and suicide
Trying otherwise to intervene	
Trying to kill	

Boys	Girls
Learn males are violent	See male violence as normal
Disrespect women	Women get no respect
Use violence in own relationships	Acceptance
Attack father or mother	Become pregnant
Confusion, insecurity about being man	
Contribute to teenage pregnancy	

Not all children are affected seriously or in the same way. The above behaviours do *not* show that children are bad; they are ways they have of *surviving or protecting themselves* in homes where there is violence.

Emergency relaxation method

It has been demonstrated indisputably that by inducing a relaxation response through meditation and proper breathing you can improve your reaction to situations that cause you stress. We will return to these issues in more detail later in the programme.

WHEN YOU ARE GETTING REALLY WORKED UP

1. Say STOP to yourself and stay still.

2. Let your shoulders and jaw drop. Open your hands and try to relax them.

3. Breathe in deeply and breathe out slowly. And again.

4. Now take two or three small, quiet breaths.

5. Can you now begin to deal with the situation in a way which will not cause harm to others or yourself?

Working between sessions

Think about your own experiences in moving from boyhood to manhood. Can you identify what were the most important things for you in becoming a 'man'?

What was it that actually made you think of yourself: 'now *I'm a man*'?

1.

2.

3.

4.

5.

What were the most difficult things for you in growing into manhood?

1.

2.

3.

Stage 1 Session 4

Objectives of session

Participants will:

1. increase awareness of how the messages they have received about their role as men may relate to their use of controlling and abusive behaviours

2. increase awareness of how power and control issues impact on their behaviour within relationships.

Outline of session

Content	Methods and process
1. Welcome and outlining of objectives	
2. Processing work done since last session	Take one factor from each participant that made them think of themselves as men and one difficulty associated with this. Put on flip chart.
3. Growing up male (1)	Group to reflect on the information about men contained in Figure 5.4 (see p.84) and to think about the links between how they have been socialised as men and the range of problem behaviours presented by large numbers of men. WHY?
	Present 'boy' – 'man' model in Figure 5.5 (see p.85) and explore the following issues:
	• How do you make the transition, how do you prove maleness, what is the cost?
	• Where do ideas about having to be hard, strong, tough come from?
	• Public v. private behaviour
	• Pressure to conform – can't cope, must cope
	• Staying in control.
	Group round in which each participant identifies links between his own experience of growing up and having to use hard, controlling-type behaviours.

Stage I Session 4 (continued)

Content	Methods and process
4. Growing up male (2)	Share and discuss hand-out 'Growing-up male (2)' (p.86).
5. Considering power and control	Work through exercise 'Thinking about power and control issues' (see p.87).
6. Gender issues and control	Participants to complete the 'What rules are you living by?' exercise. Discuss briefly within group.
	What are the links to the power and control issues just raised?
	Ask participants to think back to the self-assessment exercise in Session 2. Can they begin to see some of their behaviour not as a series of isolated and reactive incidents but as having something to do with a pattern of behaviour which is about trying to maintain or get back control?
	Are there links to the ways they have been brought up and socialised as men?
	Share quote from male perpetrator in Figure 5.6 (see p.88).
	Stress that this session is simply to get people thinking about issues concerning men and women and power and control. Conclude by pointing out that power is a complex and very liquid thing. Does one ever really have hold of it? Participants need to reflect whether they are becoming too possessive about having it – or keeping it – and if this is leading to them being more controlling at times.
	Will be able to focus in more depth in Stage 2.
7. Working between sessions	See p.90.
8. Unwinding and closure	See p.126.

Masculinity

* In school, most children with behaviour problems or learning difficulties are boys

* Most crime carried out by men

* Nearly ALL violence carried out by men

* Prison population nearly ALL men

* Suicide level higher among men

* Men routinely fail at close relationships

WHY ?

Figure 5.4. Stage 1 Session 4. Masculinity (adapted from Biddulph 1999).

Growing up male

YOUNG ➡ MALE

small	big
emotional	inexpressive
irresponsible	responsible
vulnerable	hard
inexperienced	experienced
dependent	independent
can cry	can't cry

Figure 5.5. Stage 1 Session 4. Growing up male (adapted from Murphy 1996).

Growing up male (2)

- For tens of thousands of years men lived as warriors, hunters and providers
- They were dominant over women and indispensable as bread-winners
- Strength and brawn were admired and feared
- Men's superiority was related to their physical attributes.

THE STURDY OAK

Stand alone, don't lean on anyone, the protector and provider – hard, brave and manly. Prepared to sacrifice oneself.

NO SISSY STUFF

Don't cry, don't show feelings, hard to read, don't be feminine.

THE BIG WHEEL

Successful at sport, work, in charge. Defined by what one achieves.

GIVE THEM HELL

Aggressive, slag with the best of them, compete.

BUT!

- Men know they can't live up to such standards but keep trying
- May lead to jealousy, rage and violence or depression
- Some men may get dominance and power in their lives by getting it with women.

(Adapted from David and Brannon 1976.)

Thinking about power and control issues

To begin, draw a large triangle on a flip chart. Agree with participants what it represents (any grouping or organisation within society, e.g. army, a factory, a business, etc.).

Consider following questions briefly:

- Who is at the top?

- Where are others placed?

- How do those at the bottom communicate with those higher up?

- Who has the greatest power?

- How easy is it to be straight and honest with each other?

- Whose views and way of thinking are important?

Each participant then to think about his own situation, his relationship, his family and how the power is worked out.

Are they aware of how power and control issues are being played out? What difficulties is this causing?

If there is time, encourage the men to do a triangle representing the 'power' situations within their own relationships and families.

View of a male perpetrator

'Domestic violence comes from two things:

the authority you believe you have over your wife, and the services you expect to get from her.

And both are wrong.

You do not own her.

You cannot control her, but a man who batters feels that the woman is hurting him.'

Figure 5.6. Stage 1 Session 4. View of a male perpetrator (Courtney 1997).

What rules are you living by?

Think about the expectations you have of your relationship. You need to ask yourself honestly to what extent you try to have control over your wife or partner. Do you tend to have set rules and firm ideas about things? Put your partner's name into the following statements and then read them carefully to see how many of them you have found yourself thinking or believing.

1.   I should be in charge of my own home.

2.   .... should shut up when I tell her.

3.   .... should listen to me when I'm speaking.

4.   .... should tell me where she goes and who she is with

5.   .... mustn't push me too far.

6.   If .... disobeys me I should know why.

7.   .... shouldn't do or say things which she knows make me angry.

8.   I should be able to be sexual with my wife or partner if I really want to.

9.   .... shouldn't nag me.

10.   The child/children should be mainly ....'s responsibility.

11.   .... should look after me.

12.   .... shouldn't expect me to become too involved in everything about the house.

Other things that you strongly believe:

(Adapted from Morran and Wilson 1997)

Working between sessions

A lot of men shut down their feelings in childhood and adolescence and then find it difficult to understand and manage their feelings and emotions as they experience difficulties in life.

Think about your own feelings and emotions.

- Are you aware of the range of feelings you experience?

- Which feeling or emotion gives you the most trouble?

- What feelings do you find it hardest to cope with?

Give three reasons why you think you experience difficulty with some of your feelings.

1.

2.

3.

Stage I Session 5

Objectives of session

Participants will:

1.   increase awareness of the impact of feelings and emotions

2.   increase awareness of the effects of anger and jealousy on their behaviour

Outline of session

Content	Methods and Process
1. Welcome and outlining of objectives	
2. Processing work done since last session	List on flip chart the main emotions which have been identified as difficult and one reason from each participant.
3. Exploring emotions	Ask each participant to state what feeling(s) he is having at this moment. A significant number may say something like 'OK' or 'fine' or 'bad', etc. Reflect back that they have not answered the question. They have judged how they feel, they have not actually said what they are feeling.
	Briefly work through exploring emotions, Figure 5.7, and then complete emotions brainstorm as outlined on p.94.
4. The process of anger	Stress that anger is a natural, normal emotion that we all experience. The problem is how to manage it in a healthy and non-abusive way. It can be such an energising and exhilarating emotion. However, it may seduce our minds with self-righteous inner talk that gives us convincing arguments for venting our rage.
	Share information on understanding anger in Figure 5.8 (see p.95 and guidelines on pp.94–96).
	Stress that the latest research indicates that venting anger and suppressing it are *both* harmful to our health and do not help us learn how to control it.
	'DON'T SUPPRESS IT BUT DON'T ACT ON IT' (See Figure 5.9 on p.98.)

Stage I Session 5 (continued)

Content	Methods and Process
5. Exploring jealousy	Brainstorm what jealousy is.
	Participants then to work through questionnaire 'Understanding your jealousy'. Process within group and seek to bring out following key points:
	• Jealousy can be related to expectations that some men may have of their partners with regard to love, attention, affection, respect, sex, time, etc.
	• Jealousy may also link to feelings of low self-esteem, insecurity which may be covered up with a hard front of toughness, exaggerated self-importance, wanting to be right, etc.
	• Do some men become dependent on their partners – wanting them to look up to them, to adore them, etc.?
	• Jealous behaviour must damage relationships and leave women feeling controlled, not loved, imprisoned, owned and trapped!
	Stress that this session has raised issues which will be returned to in more depth in Stage 2.
6. Working between sessions	See p.100.
7. Unwinding and closure	See guidelines, p.126.

Exploring emotions

✱ Sources of energy and power

✱ Neither good nor bad – simply ARE

✱ Feel them in our bodies

✱ Lose touch with real feelings

✱ Hide and repress true feelings

✱ Awareness and management of
feelings

CLAIM IT	NAME IT	TAME IT	AIM IT

Figure 5.7. Stage 1 Session 5. Exploring emotions.

Facilitator's guidelines on emotions brainstorm and understanding anger

Begin with a blank flip chart with a large funnel drawn on it as below. Encourage the group to come up with as wide a range of feelings and emotions as possible and write these in the funnel. Ensure that the main emotions and their derivatives are included: joy, fear, sadness, disgust, jealousy, anger and hate. Write up the negative feelings of anger, rage, jealousy, frustration, insecurity, let-down, nervousness, guilt, displeasure, dejection, feeling troubled, unhappiness, annoyance, hurt, etc. towards the narrow end of the funnel.

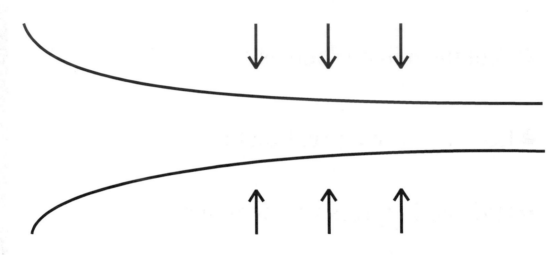

When a full list of emotions has been gathered, ask participants to begin to think about how they actually deal with their emotional life. Can they relate back to some of the pressures and expectations placed on them which they explored in the last session (e.g. macho, not showing feelings, hard to read etc.)? Add the arrows to show how these forces may squeeze emotions into the narrow end of the funnel. Is there a danger that their suppression of feelings may eventually burst out into aggressive and violent behaviour?

The process of anger

In light of the above activity, ask participants to think about how they deal with their anger. The inability to manage one's anger properly can lead to verbal or physical violent outbursts. Stress that things just don't happen, and that however quickly events appear to occur, there is a process and once you begin to understand it you may be able to do something about it.

Understanding anger

CRISIS POINT

Uncontrolled violent behaviour

MOVING UP
Getting worked up

RECOVERY

Danger of recurrence

TRIGGERS
The event or situation
viewed as negative

BASE LINE

THE DIP

Figure 5.8. Stage 1 Session 5. Understanding anger (Novacco 1976).

BASE LINE

Each person's starting-point. We are all different. Some of us are very easy going and laid back, while others are much quicker to fly off the handle, or more on edge, etc.; we need to think about our own position.

TRIGGERS

These are the prompts, the cues, the things that set us going. Highlight that it's the way we think about and appraise situations, how we weigh them up, that is the key. (We'll look more at this next week.) Reflect back on the last session and to how we see our roles and those of our partners within relationships. For example, have we a trigger around our partner criticising us?

MOVING UP

An exhilarating and energising process – getting ourselves worked up with a self-righteous inner talk that is giving us convincing arguments for venting anger, for example: 'She's a lazy bitch…she's been lying about all day phoning her friends wasting money'. Point out that the adrenalin is now starting to pump through the body and there is a definite physiological process under way, but that it is still possible to step back. Current research identifies two possible ways:

TIME OUT or CHALLENGING YOUR THINKING (TRIGGERS)

CRISIS POINT

The point at which you behave in a physically or verbally or emotionally abusive way. You are out of control. You 'blow your top', 'lose it', etc.; your body is flooded with high levels of stress-inducing chemicals and blood pressure may be raised.

RECOVERY

Starting to come back down. Be careful: adrenalin remains in the system for approximately 90 minutes, and there is a danger it will shoot back up again into a second crisis.

THE DIP

Regret, depression, feeling sorry for yourself. Trying to make up. It's not easy to talk yourself out of something you've behaved yourself into.

CONCLUSION

Highlight the main point that we have a responsibility to look at where our anger comes from and to ensure that it is not triggered by abusive and controlling attitudes and beliefs. Are you losing control in order to get control? Stress the point that abusive behaviour in relationships is not about anger. Abuse often occurs where there is no anger, or the anger may come from negative beliefs and mindsets which need to change.

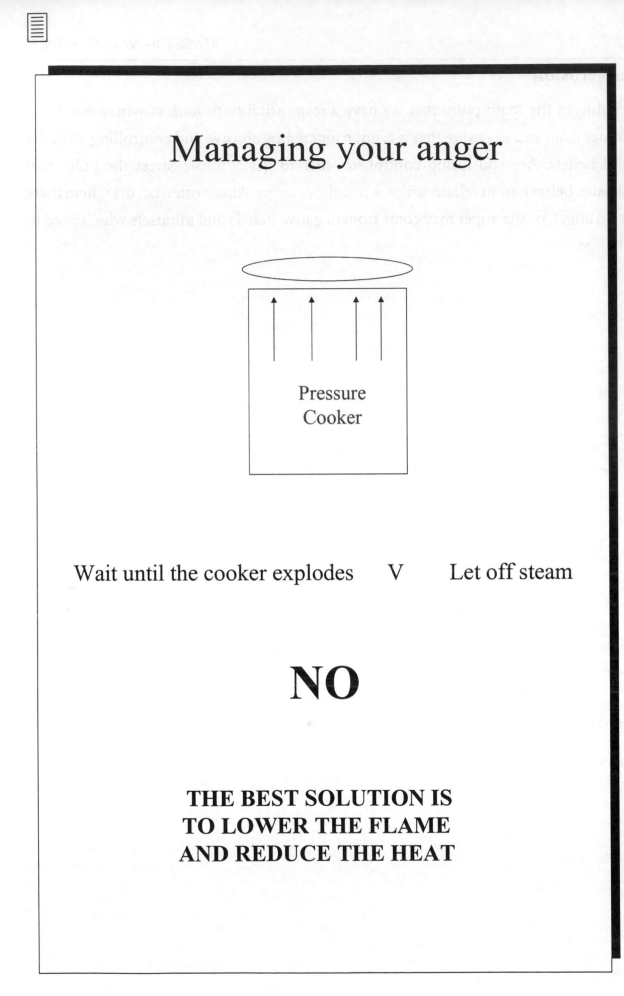

Figure 5.10. Stage 1 Session 5. Managing your anger.

Understanding your jealousy

When do you feel most jealousy towards your wife or partner?

What sort of things do you feel ought to be yours by right from your wife or partner?

Why is it difficult to talk about jealousy?

If you feel bad about yourself for being jealous, how do you cover it up?

How do you try to regain feelings of self-worth?

If you have very strong 'macho' ideas about being a man (as we talked about last week) they may make you feel more jealous. Do you agree and why do you think this is?

How does your wife or partner experience your jealousy?

How can you end up feeling better about yourself without having to put down your wife or partner?

Working between sessions

Think about two occasions in the past when you were abusive to your wife or partner and:

1.   You were feeling very angry with her

or

2.   You were feeling very jealous towards her.

Now briefly write down what you did on each occasion and in particular what you were actually *thinking*.

Situation 1:

Situation 2:

Stage 1 Session 6

Objectives of session

Participants will:

1. increase awareness of thinking and beliefs that may lead to abusive behaviour

2. increase awareness of how to control what they think and do.

Outline of session

Content	Methods and process
1. Welcome and outlining of objectives	
2. Processing work done since last session	Each participant to give an example of the thinking which came before his heightened emotion of either anger or jealousy.
3. Exploring negative thinking	Share an example of three people each behaving differently in response to the same situation. They have been waiting for the bus to work and it has just driven past them. One person reacts angrily and aggressively, one reacts passively and the third deals positively with the situation.
	Ask the group to explain why the individuals reacted differently. Bring out the importance of how each person *thought* about the situation to explain how they then felt and reacted. For example:
	Man 1: bus driver did it deliberately, he's an idiot, he's made me late for work, etc.
	Man 2: I'm going to be in trouble, nothing I can do, etc.
	Man 3: I will phone work, I can have a walk in the park, I will relax for a change, etc.
	Relate this example to the Understanding Behaviour model in Figure 5.10 (see p.103).
4. Thinking about thinking	Point out that this session will be focusing on how we think. One of the things which makes us different from animals is that we can actually think about how we think! The capacity for self-awareness allows us to work at change. To begin with, encourage participants to explore their own thinking processes. Use the 'Thinking about thinking' exercise (see p.104).

Stage 1 Session 6 (continued)

Content	Methods and process
5. Thinking and beliefs	Take participants through the example 'Relating negative thinking to abusive behaviour' (p.106) and complete this, followed by the individual exercise on p.107. Process within main group.
	As indicated at the end of the exercise, ask participants to reflect on where the man's stinking thinking may have come from. What sort of *beliefs* could he have about women and relationships in general? Brainstorm as wide a range of beliefs as possible. For example:
	• Women should look after men
	• Women cannot be trusted
	• Women are too emotional
	• Women are always moaning
	• Women keep going on and on about a problem
	• A woman shouldn't have any male friends
	• Women should trust their partner's opinion
	• The man should have the final say
	• If the man is not in charge he'll get walked over.
	Conclude by pointing out that a lot of research indicates that men who are abusive to their partners have such beliefs. These seem to be about:
	1. not fully giving themselves to a relationship, staying central and separate
	2. being in some way superior
	3. expecting to be cared for by their partners.
	These beliefs can be buried deep. Each participant needs really to explore his own mindset. Until they are able to get at their deeply ingrained way of seeing their role and relationship and put it out on the table and challenge and change it, it will be hard to move forward.
6. Positive self-talk and thinking	Highlight the importance of thinking positively if people are to move forward into change. Work through the material on 'Positive self-talk' (p.107). Each participant to share the positive statement that means most to them or that they would like to strive for.
7. Working between sessions	See p.108.
8. Unwinding and closure	See guidelines, p.126.

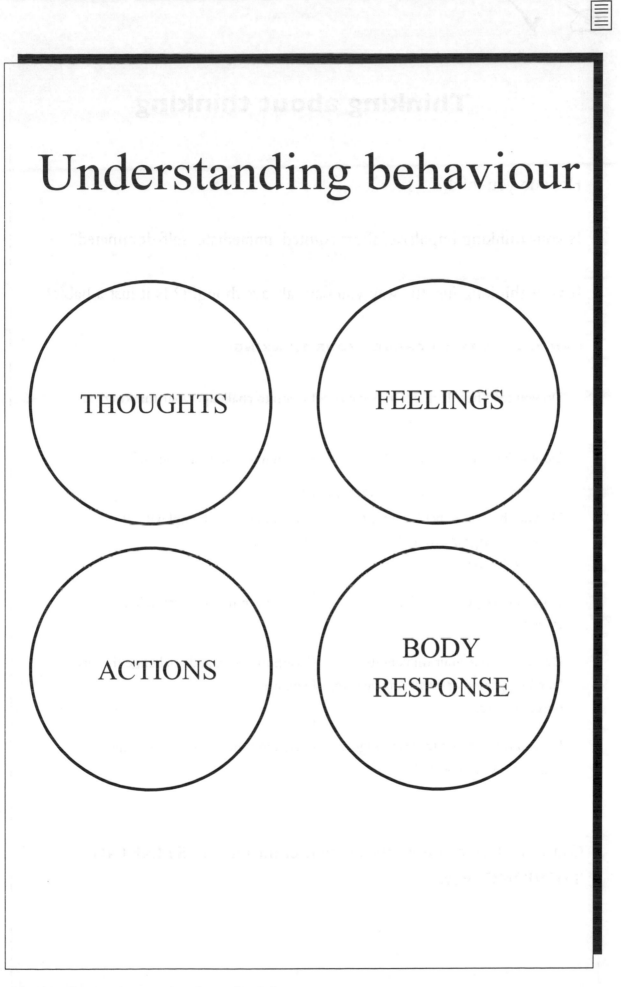

Figure 5.10. Stage 1 Session 6. Understanding behaviour.

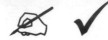

Thinking about thinking

How do you think?

Is your thinking impulsive, short-sighted, immediate, self-dominated?

Is your thinking just the way you have always thought? Is it just a habit?

CAN YOU WORK TO CHANGE YOUR THINKING?

Do you read hostile intent into even neutral actions by your wife/partner?	Learn to challenge your thinking?
Do you jump to conclusions?	Learn to consider a range of alternatives.
Do you think in either/or ways? (good/bad, right/wrong, winners/losers)	Learn to see the complexity of situations.
Do you over-generalise from one event?	Learn to think more carefully.
Do you inflame your thinking by labelling people or events in negative, obscene ways?	Learn to define and challenge the terms you use.
Do you think about things in highly negative, extreme ways?	Learn to think more realistically.

Can you relate to at least one example of the types of **STINKING THINKING** above?

Relating negative thinking to abusive behaviour

John and Ann are at the club with some friends. They are having a good time. John notices Ann talking and laughing with Peter up at the bar.

JOHN'S THINKING

She's interested in him, she's flirting, she's ignoring me, she shouldn't be that friendly to him, etc.

JOHN'S FEELINGS

Rejected, angry, outraged, jealous, flooded with strong negative emotions.

JOHN'S BODY REACTIONS

Heart beating more quickly, breathing hard, adrenalin pumping, muscles tensing, etc.

JOHN'S ACTIONS

Staring hard, pacing about, ready to pounce. etc.

Ask participants to focus on John's actual thinking processes. In what ways was his thinking flawed?

For example: jumping to conclusions, reading bad intentions into partner's behaviour, labelling, emotionalised thinking.

Where does such STINKING THINKING come from?

The critical issue is to get at the **BELIEF SYSTEM OR MINDSET** which leads to such thinking and then to abusive behaviour.

Ask participants to reflect on whether such ideas are present in their own thinking and could feed into their own behaviour. Complete the individual exercise (p.106) and share examples within the group.

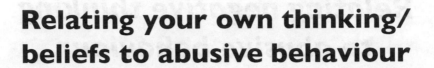

Relating your own thinking/ beliefs to abusive behaviour

Think about a recent occasion when you were abusive to your wife or partner (don't put down what she did).

What were you thinking just before you became abusive?

Can you identify any 'stinking thinking'?

Can you relate this to any negative beliefs you may have?

Can you make any changes to these beliefs or thinking?

What differences would such new thinking make to your situation?

Positive self-talk

Research and experience have shown that when people work to change their self-talk from negative to positive they feel better about themselves and become safer people to be with.

Read the following list. Tick those statements that you could agree with or wish to try to bring more into your own thinking.

- I can accept and like myself

- I can control what I do and not other people

- I can accept criticism

- I can accept that I am not right all the time

- I can feel that it is OK to walk away from a fight

- I can hear other people's anger and not feel threatened or get angry back

- It's OK to feel insecure and uncertain at times

- I don't need everyone to like me

- I don't have to rise to the bait when I think other people are trying to wind me up

- I don't have to feel I'm the centre of attention in order to feel good

- It's OK to feel scared about things at times; life can be scary

Other examples of your own positive self-talk:

- I can…

- I am able…

Working between sessions

Change is difficult. There are no quick fixes. It is an inside-out process which has to come from yourself. No one can make you change.

Identify at least three things about yourself or your behaviour that you will find difficult to change. Why is this so?

1.

2.

3.

Stage 1 Session 7

Objectives of session

Participants will:

1.   recognise the inappropriateness of quick-fix solutions

2.   increase awareness of difficult process of change.

Outline of session

Content	Methods and process
1. Welcome and outlining of objectives	
2. Processing work done since last session	Each participant to give one example of a difficult area for change. Write on flip chart and hold for later in session.
3. Quick fixes v. long-term solutions	Brainstorm various quick-fix strategies that men have used to try to put right what they have done.
	Discussion on why these haven't worked.
	What are the expectations underlying the belief in quick fix?
	Emphasise that no one can just talk their way out of situations that they have behaved themselves into.
	In fact, thinking that there are quick fixes may lead men to be more abusive, and start to put pressure on their partners. If they are sincere they will have to let trust build up slowly. Recall the long-term consequences for the victims of domestic violence covered in Session 2.
	Ask the group to think about more longer term, meaningful solutions.
	Link this to one of the quick fixes: APOLOGISE
	What are the alternatives to this? Should we forget about apologising? Do we expect to be rewarded when we apologise? What would make apologies more meaningful?

Stage 1 Session 7 (continued)

Content	Methods and process
3. Quick fixes v. long-term solutions (continued)	Group to brainstorm a list of possible, real, long-term solutions. Each participant to identify two solutions that would be important for him to focus on.
4. Exploring the process of change	Ask participants to think about an area in their life where they have ever tried to make changes, e.g. giving up smoking, drinking, chocolate, etc. Take one example and exlpore it in relation to the model outlined in Figure 5.11 (see p.111). Relate this to the difficult process of trying to move away from the use of controlling and abusive behaviours. It is a slow, hard journey.
5. Accepting responsibility	Introduce the idea of the importance of honesty and taking full responsibility for what we do if we are going to make positive changes. Consider the example of a child who breaks a window and then tries to avoid responsibility. List the excuses. Summarise these: DENIAL MINIMISING BLAMING OTHERS Each participant to complete exercise on 'Accepting responsibility' (p.113) and then feed back at least one of the ways that he has used to excuse his unacceptable behaviour. Process in main group.
6. Is change possible?	Work slowly through the summary sheet in Figure 5.13 (see p.112), stressing the key points about the difficult process of change.
7. Working between sessions	See p.114.
8. Unwinding and closure	See guidelines, p.126.

The process of change

Relapse

Keeping it going

Taking definite action

Deciding to do
something about it

Thinking about
need to change

Not thinking about need to change

?

Figure 5.11. Stage 1 Session 7. The spiral of change (adapted from Prochaska and Di Clemente 1984).

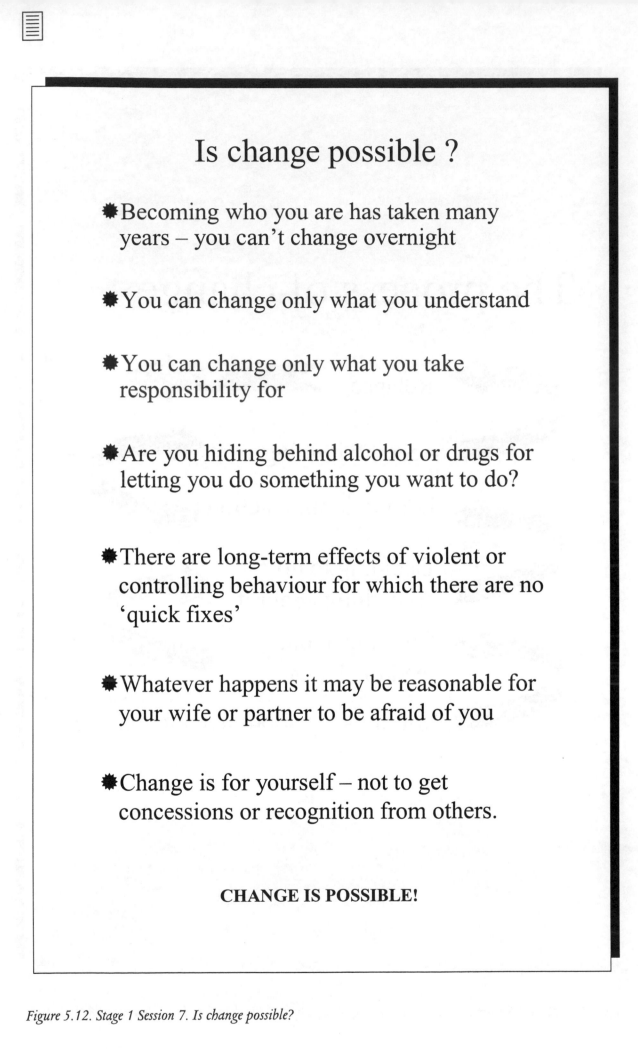

Is change possible ?

✹ Becoming who you are has taken many years – you can't change overnight

✹ You can change only what you understand

✹ You can change only what you take responsibility for

✹ Are you hiding behind alcohol or drugs for letting you do something you want to do?

✹ There are long-term effects of violent or controlling behaviour for which there are no 'quick fixes'

✹ Whatever happens it may be reasonable for your wife or partner to be afraid of you

✹ Change is for yourself – not to get concessions or recognition from others.

CHANGE IS POSSIBLE!

Figure 5.12. Stage 1 Session 7. Is change possible?

Accepting responsibility or making excuses

When you have been violent or abusive to your wife or partner, what explanations have you given for the way in which you have behaved? Look at the following examples and tick any that are similar to those you have used in the past.

I just snapped ☐

I didn't do anything wrong ☐

I don't remember doing it ☐

I didn't mean to hurt you ☐

I was acting in self-defence ☐

I'm not really violent ☐

You're making it up ☐

That's how people behave where I come from ☐

I was only trying to hold you back ☐

I hardly touched you ☐

You're exaggerating ☐

I was under a lot of pressure ☐

I only threw something at you to shut you up ☐

You bruise easily ☐

It wasn't that bad ☐

I was drunk ☐

You pushed me too far ☐

That's how my father treated my mother ☐

I just lost control ☐

You provoked me ☐

I did it to get you to do what you were told ☐

You made me jealous ☐

You hit me first ☐

I have a bad temper which I can't control ☐

You know I won't really hurt you ☐

Others...

(Adapted from Emerge 1977)

Working between sessions

1.   Is there a pattern to my violent/abusive behaviour that I can recognise? (If Yes, try to describe it in a few words.)

2.   Are there particular situations associated with my abusive behaviours?

3.   How often do I become abusive?

         Is it a matter of days or weeks or months or longer between violent outbursts?

         Is there no clear time pattern?

         Is it becoming more frequent?

4.   Where am I on this pattern right now?

5.   Has my behaviour been getting worse and in what ways?

Stage I Session 8

Objectives of session

Participants will:

1. increase awareness of their pattern or cycle of violence and how it impacts on their wife or partner

2. review their learning and progress so far

3. increase their awareness of changing responses by society to domestic violence.

Outline of session

Content	Methods and process
1. Welcome and outlining of objectives	
2. Processing work done since last session	Without going into too much detail each participant is to indicate whether or not they can see a pattern to their abusive behaviour.
3. Exploring how violence might erupt	Participants to reflect on how their behaviour brings them closer to violence. What are the kinds of situations in which they frequently get worked up? Behaviour is often habitual: we just get into a certain way of behaving (for example, do participants in the group sit on the same seat each week?) Participants also to ask themselves if they are aware of situations in which they don't feel they are getting worked up but other people would say they are. Share examples of each of the above situations.
4. Understanding the cycle of violence	Begin by looking at the aftermath of an abusive outburst. What is the first thing a man may say or do after he has been violent to his wife or partner? Is there a period of remorse? Is there a making up or 'hearts and flowers' phase?

Stage 1 Session 8 (continued)

Content	Methods and process
4. Understanding the cycle of violence (continued)	Then, as time moves on, what begins to happen? Does he begin to reappraise, maybe thinking that it was as much her fault?
	Is this the beginning of a 'fault-finding' phase? Does he seek to reassert his authority? Does tension begin to build up? Does this then lead to another outburst?
	Present cycle of violence model, Figure 5.13 (see p.117).
	Each participant to do individual exercise on the cycle and share. (p.118)
5. Northern Ireland's changing response to domestic violence	Emphasise to participants that more and more the law and courts are trying to protect victims of domestic violence. Things are changing. Can mention example of drink-driving and how there is now less tolerance towards it than there was 20 years ago. Work through hand-out 'Northern Ireland's changing response' (see p.119).
6. Review of learning	Each participant to review his notes of previous 8 sessions and complete 'Summary of learning' form (p.120). The questions highlight some of the main issues covered up to this point. Take examples from within the group.
7. Evaluating Stage 1	Ask participants to complete the 'Review of Stage 1' form, to give them the opportunity to give their views on the learning experience. This can be done in session or for the next session. Point out that the purpose of taking feedback is to help ensure that the programme is being delivered as well as possible to participants.
8. Affirmation and closure	Affirm participants for having reached this part of the course. Emphasise that they now have covered the crucial knowledge-base. With the resultant raised awareness, they need now to move forward into Stage 2 and begin to focus and work at changing their own behaviours.

The cycle of violence

Episode of abuse

Build-up
phase

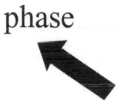

Remorse
phase

Honeymoon
period

*'A consistently repeating
cyclical pattern'*

Figure 5.13. Stage 1 Session 8. The cycle of violence (Walker 1979).

Thinking about my cycle of violence

1. Is there a cycle to my violent/abusive behaviour that I can recognise? (If Yes, try to describe it in a few words.)

2. In the past, after I was violent or abusive to my partner, what would be the first things I would say to her immediately afterwards?

3. (a) What kind of things did I say to my partner when I was in the 'hearts and flowers' phase?

    (b) What kind of things did I do when I was in the 'hearts and flowers' phase?

4. When I felt that I had done enough, how did I start fault-finding again?

    (a) What sort of things did I say?

    (b) What sort of things did I do?

5. How quickly do I seem to go from one stage to another?

    days   weeks   months   other   don't know

6. Where am I on this cycle right now?

Northern Ireland's changing response to domestic violence

Violence against women is a criminal offence.

POLICE NOW HAVE A PRO-ARREST POLICY

- They have to respond to a call
- Their priority is to protect victims
- They will enforce the law
- They support the victim
- They are more aware of domestic violence.

FAMILY HOMES AND DOMESTIC VIOLENCE (N. IRELAND) ORDER 1998

A new single code of law which improves and extends the level of protection available. Non-molestation and occupation orders now available to protect victims both at and outside the home.

Breaches of these orders are now criminal offences and police have the power of arrest.

ARTICLE 12A CHILDREN (N. IRELAND) ORDER 1995

Anyone who is subject to a non-molestation order and wants to have formal contact with their children may do so only after the court considers the risk of harm to the children as a result of them seeing or hearing ill-treatment of another person.

HARASSMENT (N. IRELAND) ORDER 1997

It is now a criminal offence to harass anyone on more than two occasions. It covers a wide range of behaviours that a normal person would see as being deliberately intrusive and involving harassment.

Everyone has the right to live without fear.

Summary of learning

It is important at this part of the programme to try to bring together what you have learnt so far so that you can build on this as you move into the main part of the course.

- What are the main types of abusive controlling behaviours that I use and that I need to work on (e.g. slapping, shouting, threatening, humiliating, etc.)?

- What do I think have been the main effects on my wife/partner?

- How has my violent and aggressive behaviour affected the children?

- What are some of the beliefs or ideas I have about myself as a man that may be connected to my controlling behaviours?

- Do I need to work with my negative feelings of anger and jealousy?

- How can I do this?

- Have I played down and not taken full responsibility for my use of controlling and aggressive behaviours?

Review of Stage I

Circle the sessions you have attended 1 / 2 / 3 / 4 / 5 / 6 / 7 / 8

1. What word(s) best describe(s) how you usually feel during sessions? (Underline as appropriate.)

    anxious   **nervous**   **uncomfortable**   **depressed**   **angry**

    calm   **relaxed**   **frustrated**   **happy**   **guilty**

    any other word(s) ....

2. How helpful have you found the programme, to date, in helping you work at your use of controlling and aggressive behaviours?

    6   **5**   **4**   **3**   **2**   **1**

    very helpful   not helpful at all

3. What do you feel have been the most helpful parts of the course to date?

4. What do you feel have been the least helpful parts of the course to date?

5. Do you complete the worksheets between sessions?

6. Can you identify any changes you need to make in your behaviour?

7. How much time do you spend thinking about the course between sessions?

6

Stage 2: Working at Change

Stage 2 is the engine-room of the programme. It builds on the motivational and educational base laid down in the first stage. Participants should now strive to work towards changing various and specific areas of their behaviour.

The 12 sessions in this stage focus on the six areas of domestic violence identified in the definition agreed in *Tackling Domestic Violence* (DHSS and NIO 1995). Two weeks are spent on each of the areas and tactics of behaviour. These are:

- Sessions 1 and 2 – physical violence
- Sessions 3 and 4 – threats and intimidation
- Sessions 5 and 6 – sexual abuse
- Sessions 7 and 8 – male privilege and economic abuse
- Sessions 9 and 10 – isolation
- Sessions 11 and 12 – emotional abuse.

Over the course of two sessions each of the above areas of behaviour is explored in detail. First, the range of behaviours that make up this kind of abuse are identified. Then, an example of the behaviour is processed in detail. Participants are next asked to look hard at their own situation and try to identify, explore and reflect on when they have used such behaviour. In particular they are encouraged to focus on:

1. The effects of my behaviour (on my partner, my children and myself)
2. The gains and losses from the use of such behaviour
3. How the behaviour can be played down, excused or blamed on someone or something else
4. The mindset or way of seeing things underpinning the use of such behaviour.

The two forms 'Exploring abusive and controlling behaviour' and 'Understanding my abusive and controlling behaviour' are used to facilitate this work. The first form is used to help participants process the particular area of behaviour while the second is used to assist them to work individually on the extent to which they use it. Example scenarios are included in the manual which can be read out to participants. Scenarios on video, purpose-made or taken from films or television, can also be helpful ways of illustrating the particular tactic under scrutiny. It is also feasible to use participants to play out some of the scenarios, and some of their own examples. The use of a more experiential approach can greatly assist the learning process and inject some energy into the group. Some care is required if using such methods. (See Appendix 2.)

Each double session finishes with a presentation and discussion of ideas and suggestions on ways of moving away from such abusive behaviours and towards positive behaviour. The goal is to move from violence to non-violence; from threatening behaviour to non-threatening, safe behaviour; from sexual selfishness towards sexual respect and intimacy; from male privilege and economic control to fairness and partnership; from isolation to support; and from emotional abuse to respect.

Stage 2 also introduces the weekly check-in process into the programme. It is important that participants begin to connect what they are doing on the programme to their own situations and have the chance to process briefly some of the behaviours that they are using. (See 'Checking in and out' guidelines, below.)

Checking In and Out
The check-in: Raising awareness and self-monitoring

During Stages 2 and 3 of the programme, all sessions will begin with each participant reflecting on the period since the previous session. He will select and outline briefly an example of his own behaviour during that period. Either:

- a situation or occasion when he acted in a controlling, aggressive and violent way with his wife or partner (if not in a relationship, he can link the behaviour to another area of his life) OR

- a situation or occasion when he could have acted in a controlling, aggressive or abusive way but did not (see Figure 6.1).

It is important that the participant focuses on how *he* thought and felt about the situation and the actual ways in which *he* behaved. While some lead-in and setting the context is necessary, it is unhelpful to allow too much focus on his wife's or partner's behaviours. (It may be necessary to remind some participants of the contract and their agreement not to disclose personal information about their partners.)

The man needs to get as far away from his relationships as possible and put the spotlight on his own behaviour. This will be difficult for some men. They will continue to focus on their partner's 'unreasonable or provocative behaviours' and their reactive 'uncontrolled' responses. Some may be unable to move much beyond taking more responsibility for their reactions. Others may be able to go further and see the underlying beliefs and mindsets relevant to understanding their aggressive behaviours. It is these that need to be addressed. A participant's growing awareness of where he is coming from – his attitudes and behaviours – may be a sign of progress.

In some situations, it may be that *within* the established pattern of bitterness and hostile interactions in a relationship, the partner's behaviour may be unreasonable. Continually reflect back to participants that it is not going to help *them* to change if they continually focus on their partner's behaviours. Also remind them of the long-lasting and negative impacts on someone who has lived with abuse and that the hurt and anger will have to be worked through.

Continue to encourage participants to focus on their *thinking, feelings, body reactions and actions*. They need to begin to see how these things come together and result in their use of controlling behaviour. They should then briefly analyse their behaviour in terms of its controlling effects (*outcomes*) as opposed to stated intentions or justifications. It will be through this difficult process only that awareness may be increased.

Other participants can be encouraged to ask questions and gently challenge the person speaking to think carefully about the effects of his behaviour and how it is impacting on his wife and children.

Remember that there is limited time for the check-in, so try to keep participants focused. Nevertheless, flexibility and discretion are required. More time may have to be taken with a particular participant one week at the expense of other members if he is upset or angry. The supportive aspect of the group may come into play on such occasions and may help a man cope with a difficult situation without the use of violence.

Change is a process rather than something that is ever completed. The check-in highlights the different stage that each man is at. It provides encouragement, challenge, alternative perspectives, information, and the opportunity for each man to relate how things are actually going in his life to his participation on the programme.

At times tedious and frustrating for the facilitator, and difficult to keep on track, this is nevertheless an important tool within the programme.

THE CHECK-OUT: UNWINDING AND CLOSURE

It is important to take a measure of where each participant is at, as each session ends. It is essential that no one leaves in an angry or aroused state, at increased risk of being aggressive to his partner. A range of check-outs can be used as long as they allow each participant to reflect on how he is feeling as he leaves the session. This can be done as a group round which may also ask participants to identify:

- one important piece of learning from the session, or

- one thing they plan to do over the next week to improve their behaviour, or

- one thing they are not sure about, or

- one thing they are struggling with, etc.

Try not to get back into any 'work'. The session is over, the work is done; this is a chance for participants to reflect on some aspect of the session, to tune into how they are feeling, and to leave. If someone is very distressed or angry, then it may be helpful to give that person some individual time after the session. It is important not to get into too much of a counselling mode, and referral to relevant resources for such matters as depression or addiction can be considered.

If the facilitator has any concerns about risk for the man's partner, these should be addressed at once as outlined in Chapter 4.

A word of caution

Finally, it is possible during Stage 2 that the men disclose serious criminal behaviour. Each participant chooses how much of his behaviour to share. It is worth reminding participants that if they disclose specific details of serious criminal behaviour (e.g. time and location of behaviour, identity of victim, etc.), there may then be an onus on you as the facilitator (indeed as a citizen) to pass on this information to the police. (See also value dilemmas, p.17 and risk issues pp.43–4 and 49.)

CHECK-IN

Think about either of the following:

✱ a situation when you acted in a controlling or violent way with your wife/partner

✱ a situation when you could have acted in a controlling or violent way, but did not

(if not in a relationship – think about another area of your life)

Remember, you have only a few minutes.

Concentrate on what **YOU** *were thinking and feeling, and what* **YOU** *did*

Figure 6.1. Stage 2. The check-in.

Exploring Abusive and Controlling Behaviour

What **ACTIONS** did John use to control Ann?

What did John want to happen in the situation? (His **INTENTIONS**)

What **BELIEFS/ATTITUDES** does John have which support his actions and intentions?

What **FEELINGS** was John having?

In what ways could John play down, or deny or blame Ann for his actions?

What were the **EFFECTS** of John's actions:

On John:

On Ann:

On the children:

How would John's past use of violence affect the situation?

(The questions on this form can be answered individually, in small groups or in the main group and put onto a flip chart.)

(Adapted from Pence and Paymar 1993)

Understanding my Abusive and Controlling Behaviour

Briefly outline below an example of your behaviour:

Now think about the period just before and during the time you used the above behaviour.

What were you **THINKING**?

What were you **FEELING**?

What were your **BODY REACTIONS**?

What were your **ACTIONS**?

List your immediate **GAINS** from your behaviour:

How do you think the behaviour impacted on and **affected your partner and your children**?

How did you blame your partner for what you did, or play down what you did, or in some other way **not take full responsibility** for your behaviour?

Stage 2 Session 1

Objectives of session

Participants will:

1. increase their awareness of the use of physical violence within relationships

2. explore their use of such behaviour.

Outline of session

Content	Methods and process
1. Welcome and outlining of objectives	
2. Check-in	See guidelines, pp.124–25. As this is the first 'Check-In' take some time to explain and discuss.
3. Introducing the tactic of physical violence: 'The assault'	Explain that there is a large body of research to indicate that a significant number of men use actual physical violence in their relationships (could show Fig. 5.1 on p.60) Explain that over the next two weeks the focus will be on the use of these acts that are carried out with the intention of causing physical pain or injury to another person. Group to brainstorm the range of physically violent behaviours (list on p.68).
4. Exploring an example of this behaviour	Read out 'The assault' example. Group to process man's behaviour using the form 'Exploring my abusive and controlling behaviour' (see p.128).
5. Exploring the use of violence in more detail	Group to brainstorm the immediate gains for someone who uses violence. Ensure the following go on flip chart: • reduces bodily tensions and anxiety • puts temporary end to uncomfortable situation • immobilises the woman – gets her to do what you want.

Stage 2 Session 1 (continued)

Content	Methods and process
5. Exploring the use of violence in more detail (continued)	Work through the 'Exploring the use of physical violence' sheet (on p.133). Spend some time looking at the stages of a violent episode. Can participants see any connections with their own use of violent behaviour?
6. Exploring participants' behaviours	Participants to think about their own situations. Can they relate any of their own behaviour to what has been talked about? Encourage each participant to share within the group whether he can identify with the behaviour and to briefly indicate a relevant example (if he wishes). Participants to think more about their examples for the next session, when they will have the opportunity to work at them in more detail.
7. Unwinding and closure	See guidelines, p.126.

'The assault': an example of the use of physically abusive behaviour

John and Ann have been arguing over whether to go to Spain for a holiday. John wants to go ahead because he feels he can get a good bargain at the moment which may not come up again. Ann wants to wait a while, as there are a lot of expenses coming up for the family – getting the children's rooms done up, a new washing machine, etc. (John and Ann have two children; Peter aged 8 and Jane aged 6.)

One evening, when the children have been put to bed, John and Ann are sitting in their living room.

John: 'I've decided to go ahead and book the holiday. I was talking to someone about it today.'

Ann: 'Don't be stupid. We talked about this before. We can't afford to go now. I want to get the kids' rooms done.'

John: *(interrupting and with voice raised)* 'Look, I've had a hard day at work. Don't start going on and yapping about this…You'll enjoy it too. You're always moaning and worrying about things and thinking the worst.'

Ann: 'You know we can't afford it yet. You're putting us under pressure. Why not wait a while until next year?'

John: *(staring hard at Ann and shouting)* 'Will you shut up about it. You're talking shit. I've decided and that's that.'

Ann: 'It's you who wants the holiday. It suits you. That's you all over – you decide and do things and it doesn't matter what I want.'

John then gets up from his seat and goes over to Ann. He leans over her. He slaps her across the face twice, shouting at her:

'Now will you shut up and give my head peace. I need to get out of here to get my head showered.'

Exploring the use of physical violence

What is violence?

You need to begin to be able to see violence as something which is **deliberate, intentional and used to get power and control over a person or situation**.

It is *not* a mystery.

It is *not* blind rage.

It is *not* natural.

Can you relate an occasion when you have used violence to the following stages?

- When your expectation of authority was being defied?

- When you were afraid that services which you expect were not being provided?

- When you realised that you were not going to get what you wanted?

You then decided to:

- see your potential victim as an object

- move towards her and prepare to chase and use violence

- actually use physically violent behaviour

- stop when you felt that enough violence had been used.

Can you relate to any of these stages?

(Adapted from Manalive; Men's Programme 1990)

Stage 2 Session 2

Objectives of session

Participants will:

1. explore the extent and pattern of their use of physically violent behaviour

2. identify ways to avoid the future use of such behaviour.

Outline of session

The contents	Methods and process
1. Welcome and outlining of objectives	
2. Check-in	See guidelines, pp.124–25.
3. Processing relevant examples of physically violent behaviour	Each participant to think about and reflect on a related example of his own behaviour, using the 'Understanding my abusive and controlling behaviour' form on p.129.
	With participants' agreement process one or more examples. Then group to briefly brainstorm a gains–losses analysis of the use of physically violent behaviour.
4. Further exploration of physical violence	Stress to participants that all available research tells us that the best indicator of future behaviour is past behaviour. If participants have started using physical violence in their relationships then there is a real danger that it will be repeated and also get worse. If participants are going to succeed in moving away from such behaviour they need first of all to understand the place it has already taken in their lives.

Stage 2 Session 2 (continued)

The contents	Methods and process
4. Further exploration of physical violence (continued)	Each participant to reflect on the following questions in relation to the use of physical violence:
	How often have they carried out these behaviours? Are they minimising physical violence by only thinking of it as 'just a push or a slap' (research has shown that men often play down the level of violence they use). How extreme has the behaviour been? Has their behaviour changed in type, frequency or severity over time?
5. Moving towards non-violence	Can participants commit themselves to ensuring that they will not use any further physical violence in their relationship?
	Each participant to identify three things they could work at or do to ensure that their behaviour does not escalate into physical violence, or that they do not use physical violence again. Put list on flip chart.
	Return to example(s) of abusive behaviour discussed earlier and agree how the scene could have been played out in a way in which physical violence was not used.
6. Unwinding and closure	See guidelines, p.126.

Stage 2 Session 3

Objectives of session

Participants will:

1. increase awareness of the use of threatening/intimidatory behaviours

2. explore their use of such behaviours.

Outline of session

Content	Methods and process
1. Welcome and outlining of objectives	
2. Check-in	See guidelines, pp.124–25.
3. Introducing the tactic of intimidation: 'the tightrope'	Stress to participants that if they succeed in not using physical violence, there is a real danger that they will use more subtle forms of controlling behaviour. Threats (direct or indirect) may continue or even get worse so that partners still live in fear.
	Group to begin by brainstorming range of intimidatory/threatening behaviours (see list, p.69).
4. Exploring an example of this behaviour	Read out scenario below.
	Group to process man's behaviour using the 'Exploring abusive and controlling behaviour' form (see p.128).
5. Exploring the use of threatening behaviour in more detail	Address the following questions within the group:
	What are the gains and losses of such behaviour?
	What purpose does it serve?
	Can you be threatening without being aware of it?
6. Exploring participants' behaviours	Participants to think about their own situations. Can they relate any of their behaviours to what has been talked about? Encourage each participant to share within the group whether he can identify with the behaviour and to briefly indicate a relevant example (if he wishes).
	Participants to think more about their examples for the next session, when they will have the opportunity to work at them in more detail.
7. Unwinding and closure	See guidelines, p.126.

The tightrope: an example of threatening and intimidatory behaviour

John has been working all day. Ann is at home with their two children. John returns home having had a tough day at work. When he gets in he notices that the kids' school things are lying in the hall and their toys are all over the place. Ann is on the phone talking to a friend. The dinner has not yet been started. When Ann finishes her phone call about 20 minutes later, she goes towards the kitchen and asks John how his day has been.

John: 'It's been desperate, and now I have to come into this mess and you're gabbing away on the phone.'

Ann: 'Look, I haven't been feeling too well today.'

John: 'For God's sake, it didn't stop you nattering away to your friend and running up our phone bill. What the hell have you been doing all day?'

(John stares hard at Ann)

Ann: 'Stop getting at me, will you John?'

John gets up and walks over to Ann and stands above her:

'Look, don't ever let the house get into such a mess again. You've had all day to sort it out.'

John points at her and says in a low and menacing voice:

'And in future, I want my dinner to be ready when I come in. It's not too much to ask. Do you fucking understand me?'

Stage 2 Session 4

Objectives of session

Participants will:

1. explore the extent and pattern of their use of threatening behaviour

2. identify ways to avoid the future use of such behaviour.

Outline of session

Content	Methods and process
1. Welcome and outlining of objectives	
2. Check-in	See guidelines, pp.124–25.
3. Processing relevant examples of threatening behaviour	Each participant to think about and reflect on a related example of his own behaviour using 'Understanding my abusive and controlling behaviour' form on p.129. With participants' agreement process one or more examples.
	Then group to briefly brainstorm a gains–losses analysis of the use of threatening and intimidatory behaviour.
4. Exploring the behaviour in more detail	Participants to consider their pattern in using threatening and intimidatory behaviour.
	For example, does it happen when they feel pressurised or challenged by their partners? Could they sometimes be doing it in ways that they are not fully aware of? Any examples? How often? How extreme? Has behaviour changed? It is critical that participants focus on the controlling *effects* of their actions as opposed to their stated intentions or justifications.

Stage 2 Session 4 (continued)

Content	Methods and process
5. Identifying non-threatening behaviours	Participants to brainstorm actual behaviours that demonstrate that someone is behaving in a non-threatening way. Ensure that the following go up on the flip chart:

Posture: Relaxed body, drop and extend arms with hands open.
Better to sit down.
Stay still, slow movements.

Position: Not too close, create more space.

Listening: Good eye contact (not staring intently), avert gaze, nodding, allow partner to finish.

Talking: (Not shouting), lower voice tone, using respectful language.

Content	Methods and process
6. Dealing with difficult situations	Use flip chart or overhead to take participants slowly through a difficult or conflict-type situation in an assertive way (see p.140). Allow time for discussion. Indicate that argument and conflict will be returned to in Stage 3.
7. Unwinding and closure	See guidelines, p.126.

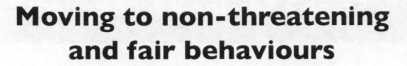

Moving to non-threatening and fair behaviours

THE DIFFICULT SITUATION

FIGHT   OR   FLIGHT

DEAL WITH IT IN AN   DEAL WITH IT
AGGRESSIVE WAY   IN A PASSIVE
                                                         WAY

DO IT MY WAY!   DO IT YOUR
                                                         WAY!

IS THERE A BETTER MIDDLE WAY?

SAY WHAT YOU THINK/FEEL IN A WAY WHICH DOES NOT
ABUSE OR CONTROL YOUR PARTNER

BE PREPARED TO CHALLENGE YOUR OWN THINKING

CAN YOU AGREE TO DISAGREE?

(Adapted from Goldman 1996)

Stage 2 Session 5

Objectives of session

Participants will:

1.   increase awareness of use of sexually abusive behaviours in relationships

2.   explore their use of such behaviour.

Outline of session

Content	Methods and process
1. Welcome and outlining of objectives	
2. Check-in	See guidelines, pp.124–25.
3. Introducing the tactic of sexually abusive behaviour – 'the object'.	Indicate to participants that there is research to show that in abusive relationships sexual violence can be more the rule than the exception.
	Stress that it is important that participants reflect on this area of their lives and examine carefully their actual behaviours.
	Group to begin by brainstorming range of behaviours that are sexually abusive within a relationship (see list, p.70).
4. Exploring an example of the behaviour	Read out scenario below. Participants to process man's behaviour using 'Exploring abusive and controlling behaviour' form. (see p.128).
5. Exploring sexually abusive behaviour in more detail	Three issues for consideration by participants:
	1. There is some evidence that a man's sexual urge is more regular, automatic and insistent than a woman's. Also, for some, the effects of growing up into manhood in a harsh, competitive and macho environment can create a numbness and lack of awareness as to how men are feeling. A deep sense of loneliness may be present and for some men sex may become the main way in which they can feel intimate and close to someone.
	These factors may lead some men to putting pressure on their partner for sex.

141

Stage 2 Session 5 (continued)

Content	Methods and process
	2. Some men want or demand sex with their partners after an abusive incident. Women say that they tend to submit out of fear that their partners will be violent again if they refuse. The man may believe that sexual intimacy is in some way making up for the violence. Explore the negative consequences of such behaviour. Causing confusion? A further degradation? Allowing man to think things are OK?
	3. Participants to reflect on society's and their use of pornographic material. How do the sexual images and fantasies affect their own sexuality and men's views of their partners' sexuality? May the result for some men be further sexual pressure on their partners?
6. Exploring participants' behaviours	Acknowledge the sensitive and private nature of the subject under consideration. Men not to give personal details involving wife or partner. Encourage each participant to share within the group whether he can identify with the behaviour and to briefly indicate a relevant example (if he wishes). Participants to think more about their examples for the next session, when they will have the opportunity to work at them in more detail.
7. Unwinding and closure	See guidelines, p.126.

'The object': an example of sexually abusive behaviour

John comes home after working a long day and having a couple of pints with his mate. He and Ann have been going through a bad patch in their relationship over the past few weeks. He slapped Ann across the face during an argument recently and they have not been sexual. John has been feeling more and more frustrated.

After John arrives home, he sits and watches some TV with Ann. They talk a bit and things seem OK. Ann goes on up to bed and John joins her shortly afterwards. He tries to arouse her. Ann says she is tired and does not want to do it tonight. John continues to touch and feel Ann and says that it has been a long time since they had sex.

'You're my wife and it's not too much to ask, it will show you how much I love you and how sorry I am.'

He continues touching Ann. She says that she does not want to. She does not physically resist him. John has sexual intercourse with Ann.

Stage 2 Session 6

Objectives of session

Participants will:

1.   explore the extent and pattern of their use of sexually abusive behaviour

2.   identify ways to avoid the future use of such behaviour.

Outline of session

Content	Methods and process
1. Welcome and outlining of objectives.	
2. Check-in	See guidelines, pp.124–25.
3. Processing relevant examples of sexually abusive behaviour	Each participant to think about and reflect on a related example of his own behaviour, using the 'Understanding my abusive and controlling behaviour' form on p.129.
	With participants' agreement process one or more examples.
	Then, group to briefly brainstorm a gains–losses analysis of use of sexually abusive behaviour.
4. Exploring attitudes about sexuality	Use questionnaire below to assist participants to reflect further on their views and attitudes with regard to sexual matters.
	Are there expectations or mindsets which may underlie the use of sexually controlling and coercive behaviours?
	Discuss in group.

Stage 2 Session 6 (continued)

Content	Methods and process
5. Exploring issues around pregnancy	Inform participants of the findings of research that shows that pregnant women can actually be at higher risk of violence from their partners. Group to brainstorm and explore why this may be the case. Facilitator to ensure that following issues are addressed: • sexual frustration • increased demands on man • behavioural changes in woman • jealousy • lack of sensitivity to woman's needs • not wanting child. Again this is an area that should be handled sensitively.
6. Moving towards sexually respectful relationships	Ask each person to identify what he feels is the most important element in a sexually respectful relationship. What does it actually mean to be sexually respectful with a partner? List these ideas about moving towards more positive behaviours within the sexual side of relationships.
7. Unwinding and closure	See guidelines, p.126.

Exploring attitudes about sexuality

Circle the numbers which best indicate your position on each view

| Men have to have sex | 1 2 3 4 5 | Men can take sex or leave it |

WHY?

| Sex should be regularly available within a relationship | 1 2 3 4 5 | The amount of sex within a relationship needs to be talked about and agreed |

WHY?

| If a heterosexual man sees an 'attractive' woman he will feel aroused | 1 2 3 4 5 | A man decides if he is going to become aroused |

WHY?

| Plenty of sex is good for you | 1 2 3 4 5 | It's more important to feel close to someone |

WHY?

| It is not important to be in a relationship to have good sex | 1 2 3 4 5 | Sex isn't enjoyable unless it's part of a good relationship |

WHY?

| Women enjoy being 'pursued and conquered' | 1 2 3 4 5 | Both parties need to be active and receptive to taking part in sex |

WHY?

| Pornography is good for sex and relationships | 1 2 3 4 5 | Pornography makes you see women as objects and harms relationships |

WHY?

Stage 2 Session 7

Objectives of session

Participants will:

1. increase awareness of the use of economic control and male privilege
2. explore their use of such behaviour.

Outline of session

Content	Methods and process
1. Welcome and outlining of objectives	
2. Check-in	See guidelines, pp.124–25.
3. Introducing tactic of economic control and use of male privilege: 'the boss'.	Explain to participants that women in abusive situations often indicate problems in how major decisions are made and the control of money within the relationship and family. Some men believe that with regard to the really big decisions, someone has to be in charge: 'You can't have two captains of a ship'. Some believe and act as if they are the king of the castle. Participants need to look closely at their behaviours in this area and see to what extent they may be controlling and abusive. Group to brainstorm the list of behaviours that may contribute to this area of abuse (see list, pp.70–71).
4. Exploring an example of this behaviour	Read out scenario below. Participants to process using the 'Exploring abusive and controlling behaviours' form on p.128.
5. Exploring male privilege in more detail	Participants to complete questionnaire below and then process in the group. Are there areas in which they are expecting to have the main say when it should be a joint decision? Are there areas where they are expecting to have a say in the decision when it should be their partner's right to choose?
6. Exploring participants' behaviours	Participants to think about their own situations. Can they relate any of their own behaviours to what has been talked about? Encourage each participant to share within the group whether he can identify with the behaviour and to briefly indicate a relevant example (if he wishes).
7. Unwinding and closure	See guidelines, p.126.

The 'boss' making decisions:
an example of the use of male privilege

John and Ann are having a pizza and watching a video. During a break Ann says that she is going to start the night class in word-processing she always hoped to do.

John looks annoyed. 'I thought we agreed last year that it wasn't worth the effort.'

Ann replies that she has been talking about the course, to one of her friends, who then got a part-time job.

'Look, if you start having to go out one night a week, who is going to mind the kids if I have to work late? There is no way you can go out to work, anyway. It'll cost too much to get child minders. You're being stupid about this…'

Ann says that it is something she would really like to do and that they could work it out.

'For God's sake, you'll be wasting your time anyway. How could you get a job when you can't even keep the house clean and organise the kids sometimes? What are you going to do anyway? Run your own business?

Ann feels very angry and disappointed. She sees how difficult John is going to be. She says just to forget about it, then, and she won't go.

'Look, I didn't say you couldn't go, did I, I just need to think about it!

Making the major decisions

Consider the following areas and think about how the decisions are made within your relationship. Tick the way that you feel your decisions are made. Is it a jointly negotiated and shared decision, do you decide, or does your partner decide?

	BOTH DECIDE	YOU DECIDE	PARTNER DECIDES
Managing your incomes	☐	☐	☐
Buying a car	☐	☐	☐
Buying a TV/video	☐	☐	☐
Buying a washing machine	☐	☐	☐
Changing your job	☐	☐	☐
Your partner changing her job	☐	☐	☐
Disciplining the children	☐	☐	☐
Child-care arrangements	☐	☐	☐
Doing housework	☐	☐	☐
Watching TV	☐	☐	☐
You taking up a new interest/activity	☐	☐	☐
Your partner taking up a new interest/activity	☐	☐	☐
Your friends	☐	☐	☐
Your partner's friends	☐	☐	☐
Moving home	☐	☐	☐

Now reflect on the following two questions:

Do you feel you are controlling most of the main decisions?

Do you feel you are opting out of major decisions and leaving much of the responsibility with your partner?

Adapted from Emerge (1997)

Stage 2 Session 8

Objectives of session

Participants will:

1. explore the extent and pattern of use of male privilege and economic control

2. identify ways to avoid the use of such behaviour.

Outline of session

Content	Methods and process
1. Welcome and outlining of objectives	
2. Check-in	See guidelines, pp.114–15.
3. Processing participants' examples	Each participant to think about and reflect on a related example of his own behaviour using the 'Understanding my abusive and controlling behaviour form' (see p.129).
	What are you doing that lets your partner know that you're the boss?
	With participants' agreement process one or more examples. Then group to briefly brainstorm a gains–losses analysis of the use of male privilege and economic control.
4. Exploring male privilege in more detail	Participants to discuss the traditional roles given to the following:
	FATHER
	HUSBAND
	MOTHER
	WIFE
	How do any of these traditional roles still play out in terms of participants' attitudes, beliefs and behaviours within their relationships?
	Are there tensions in how they see their roles and what is actually happening in their lives?

Stage 2 Session 8 (continued)

Content	Methods and process
4. Exploring male privilege in more detail (continued)	Participants to work individually at the 'Blocks to partnership' form below to seek to identify any unrealistic expectations which they may have about roles.
5. Moving towards sharing responsibility and partnership	Point out to participants that there is research to show that some men who are abusive within relationships have beliefs about being in charge and dominant but at the same time expect to be cared for and nurtured by their partners.
	Stress that male privilege is not granted by nature, God, or chromosomal difference. Such ideas have been built into the structure of society and still remain in the minds of some people.
	Participants to identify at least one area within their relationship that they need to work on, either to allow a more equal sharing of responsibility or to show a greater commitment to meeting their own responsibilities.
6. Negotiating areas of difficulty	Acknowledge that across a range of issues there will be difficulties in any relationship and no quick fixes.
	Caring for and disciplining children, managing money and sexual behaviour can all be areas of contention. There needs to be a more positive mindset in terms of a commitment to equality and an acceptance of sometimes being able to agree to disagree and find a way of trying to resolve conflicts.
	Group to brainstorm skills and guidelines which would be helpful in trying to negotiate difficult problems with partners (see 'Negotiating difficult issues', below).
	Inform participants that they will be returning to conflict-resolution issues in Stage 3 of the course. The key factor is not so much the skills involved, but the commitment to greater equality and partnership.
7. Unwinding and closure	See guidelines, p.126.

Blocks to partnership

List two expectations that you have of yourself as a partner and/or a father that you feel may be unrealistic.

What can you do to change these?

Name at least one expectation that you have of your partner that is unrealistic.

What can you do to change this now or in a future relationship?

For fathers/stepfathers: name an unrealistic expectation you have of your children

Think of two things you can do to change this unrealistic expectation

Negotiating difficult issues

PREPARATION

Are you committed to a fair process?

Are you ready:

- to listen?
- to reach an agreement which both you and your partner can live with?
- to hear things you disagree with or find hurtful without becoming abusive?
- to accept that something will change?

SETTING SOME GUIDELINES

No yelling

Don't bring up unrelated issues

No threats or intimidation

No mind games

Do you need a time limit?

Do you need a third party?

WHAT EXACTLY IS THE PROBLEM?

What is being negotiated? Is it negotiable?

How do you and also how does your partner see the problem? (This will be different for each person)

Who else is affected and in what ways?

WHAT ARE THE GOALS?

Short term: what needs to be included for an immediate solution?

Long term: what needs to be included for a final solution?

FINDING A SOLUTION

Can you find an answer that meets the needs of both parties and really improves the situation?

Is a compromise necessary?

Stage 2 Session 9

Objectives of session

Participants will:

1. increase awareness of use of isolating and non-supporting behaviours

2. explore their use of such behaviour.

Outline of session

Content	Methods and process
1. Welcome and outlining of objectives	
2. Check-in	See guidelines, pp.124–25.
3. Introducing the tactic of using isolating behaviours: 'quarantined'	Explain to participants that some perpetrators of domestic violence use acts which are intended to impose isolation on a woman, cutting her off from a community, from people, ideas or resources.
	A common theme in abusive relationships is the attempt by the man to increase his wife's dependency on him and to try to limit and restrict her access to a range of other experiences within her life.
	Participants to begin by brainstorming the types of behaviours that cause isolation (see list, p.71).
4. Exploring an example of this behaviour	Read out the scenario below.
	Group to process the man's behaviour using the 'Exploring abusive and controlling behaviour' form (see p.128).
5. Looking at isolation in more detail	Share and discuss hand-out 'Thinking more about behaviours' (below).
6. Exploring own behaviour	Participants to think about their own situations. Can they relate their behaviour to what has been talked about?
	Encourage each participant to share within the group whether he can identify with the behaviour and to briefly indicate a relevant example (if he wishes).
7. Unwinding and closure	See guidelines, p.126.

Quarantined: an example of the use of isolating behaviours

Ann and her friend have gone to their keep-fit class. John wasn't too happy about it but had reluctantly agreed. Ann arrives in at 11 o'clock. John has had a tough night with the kids. The class was due to finish at 9 but Ann had phoned to say she was going round to a friend's house for a drink. When she comes in John jumps up.

'**What the hell kept you? The kids were mustard and I've been cracking up!**'

'Look, I phoned to say I was going round to see Kate for a chat,' Ann replies tersely.

'**What did you go round to see that stupid bitch for, she's a waste of space! You should be back here helping with the kids instead of talking rubbish with her. I knew going out to this stupid keep-fit class would cause trouble.**'

John's arms are folded, he is standing close to Ann and restricting her space.

Ann feels frustrated and upset. 'Look John, I'm sick of the third degree. I can spend an hour or two with my friend if I want...'

'**That's all you think about, you just run out to your class and your friends. You're a selfish bitch, you couldn't care less about the kids; I don't think you should go out to that class again or if you do you should make sure you're back here before 9.15.**'

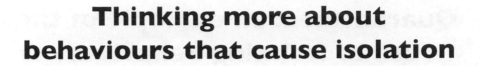

Thinking more about behaviours that cause isolation

Isolation is not a behaviour but the result of many kinds of abusive behaviours. Isolating your wife or partner involves any attempt to control whom she sees, what she does, what she wants for herself, what she thinks, or how she feels.

Peter: 'Mary was the life of the party when I met her, always planning parties, organising things – shopping trips, nights out, activities; you know, the one who got things going. I liked that about her at the start. Once we got married I wanted her to stop doing that. I don't know why exactly. I just started pressurising her to stop. Now I can't get her out of the house. I got what I wanted but now I don't want it anymore. She's lost her self-confidence. She takes the kids to things but she doesn't do stuff on her own any more.

EXAMPLES OF BEHAVIOURS THAT CAUSE ISOLATION

- Preventing or discouraging her from having certain friends
- Trying to keep her from getting involved in outside activities
- Listening to her phone conversations and reading her mail
- Not having a telephone
- Making her dependent on you for transportation
- Checking up on her
- Acting jealous or possessive whenever she's around men, accusing her of flirting
- Keeping her from going to women's meetings.

(Adapted from Pence and Paymar 1993)

Stage 2 Session 10

Objectives of session

Participants will:

1. explore the extent and pattern of their use of isolating behaviours

2. identify ways to avoid the future use of such behaviours.

Outline of session

Content	Methods and process
1. Welcome and outlining of objectives	
2. Check-in	See guidelines, p.124–25.
3. Processing participants' examples	Each participant to think about and reflect on a related example of his own behaviour using the 'Understanding my abusive and controlling behaviour' form (see p.129).
	Have you ever made your partner feel that she was being quarantined?
	With participants' agreement process one or more examples. Then group to briefly brainstorm a gains–losses analysis of the use of isolating and non-supporting behaviours.
4. Exploring isolation in more detail: possessiveness and jealousy	Each participant to identify at least three things he experiences in himself when he has feelings of jealousy towards his wife or partner: something he may be thinking, or a way he may be feeling, or something he does.
	Participants to work through 'Jealousy and domestic violence' sheet below and discuss in group.
5. Moving towards trust and support	Each participant to identify at least one way in which he could demonstrate more trust in and support for his partner, for example: • supporting one of her goals in her life • respecting her right to her own friends • respecting her right to her own opinions. Put up list on flip chart and discuss.
6. Unwinding and closure	See guidelines, p.126.

Jealousy and domestic violence

- The biggest cause of violence and murder within relationships is sexual jealousy, and almost always the man's.

- Some men beat and kill their wives or girlfriends to punish them for real or imagined unfaithfulness and to deter them from becoming unfaithful or leaving them.

- An extremely jealous man may imprison his wife in the house and interpret every incoming phone call as proof that she is unfaithful.

- Women are most at risk when they threaten to leave or do so.

- A forsaken man may stalk her, hunt her down, and execute her.

'IF I CAN'T HAVE HER, NO ONE CAN!'

For every killing of every estranged girlfriend or wife, there must be thousands of threats made by men which they might just be crazy enough to carry out, regardless of the cost.

WHY?

In what ways are the above points linked to the fact that some men still see their partners as being their *property or possessions* and an essential part of their own status and sense of importance?

(Pinker 1997)

Stage 2 Session 11

Objectives of session

Participants will:

1. increase awareness of the use of verbally and emotionally abusive behaviours

2. explore their use of such behaviour.

Outline of session

Content	Methods and process
1 Welcome and outlining of objectives	
2. Check-in	See guidelines, p.124–25.
3. Introducing the tactic of verbal and emotional abuse: 'the put-down'.	Emphasise to participants that this is often the base or foundation upon which other abusive behaviours rest. It's the most common form of control used by men. Many women report that such behaviour occurs often and may be punctuated by acts of physical violence.
	Group to brainstorm the sorts of behaviours that go to make up verbal and emotional abuse (see list, p.72).
4. Exploring an example of this behaviour	Read out the scenario below. Participants to process the man's behaviour using the 'Exploring abusive and controlling behaviour' form (see p.128).
5. Exploring the use of emotionally abusive behaviour in more detail	Participants to brainstorm the range of insults used against women and to explore the effects of such name calling on their partners. For example:
	Stupid feels unloved

Stage 2 Session 11 (continued)

Content	Methods and process
	Cunt feels angry
	Fat bitch feels unwanted
	Ugly feels unattractive
	Whore feels resentful
	Etc.

What are the undertones of such insults and what do they say about how women are viewed?

Content	Methods and process
6. Exploring the use of 'slagging' and put-downs by men	Participants to think back to the session in Stage 1 which looked at the process of growing up male.
	Think about the use of 'slagging' and verbal abuse between men in order to get at each other. Is such behaviour continuing within their relationships as a way of handling disagreement, conflict or just getting partners to behave in ways they want?
7. Exploring participants' behaviours	Participants to think about their own situations. Can they relate any of their own behaviour to what has been talked about?
	Encourage each participant to share within the group whether he can identify with the behaviour and to briefly indicate a relevant example (if he wishes).
8. Unwinding and closure	See guidelines, p.126.

The put-down: an example of the use of verbally and emotionally abusive behaviours

John and Ann are sitting watching TV. The children are up in bed. Ann is having problems with one of the neighbour's children.

'That wee lad next door knocked Peter over today and near wrecked him.'

John is flicking through the channels with the remote and not really paying attention.

Ann continues, 'I shouted at him and he gave me a real dirty look.'

John grunts.

'He's a cheeky wee shit, I'm going to have to say something to him before he hurts one of the kids…'

'Aye, OK,' mumbles John.

'Are you not worried about the kids?'

John is watching something on the TV and doesn't answer.

'Aren't you listening to me?' shouts Ann.

'What are you yapping on about now? I just want some peace and quiet. The kids are only bloody playing. You're paranoid the way you go on, you stupid bitch. You should spend less time sitting on your fat backside nosying out the window. You're not bloody wise sometimes. It does my head in having to listen to the shit you come out with.'

Stage 2 Session 12

Objectives of session

Participants will:

1. explore the extent and pattern of their use of verbally and emotionally abusive behaviour

2. identify ways to avoid the future use of such behaviour.

Outline of session

Content	Methods and process
1. Welcome and outlining of objectives	
2. Check-in	See guidelines, p.124–25.
3. Processing participants' examples	Each participant to think about and reflect on a related example of his behaviour using the 'Understanding my abusive and controlling behaviour' form (see p.129).
	With participants' agreement process one or more examples.
	Then group to briefly brainstorm a gains–losses analysis of the use of verbally and emotionally abusive behaviour.

Stage 2 Session 12 (continued)

Content	Methods and process
5. Exploring respectful communication	Participants to identify actual signs that make them aware that someone is caring about and respecting what they are saying. Ensure that the following are covered: *Verbal*: listening, asking questions, not interrupting, responding to what is being said, staying on topic, compliments, laughter at humour, reflecting back, etc. *Non-verbal*: eye contact, nodding head and showing interest, not being distracted by TV, not walking away, etc.
6. Moving towards respect in relationships	Participants to work on 'Showing respect in my relationship' form (below). Each participant to share at least one specific area that they need to work on to show more respect to their wife or partner.
7. Preparing for Stage 3	Review the six areas of behaviour covered over the past 12 weeks. Are participants able to state briefly what they need to do in each area to move towards positive behaviour in their relationship? Use the form 'Preparing for Stage 3' (below). (This may be continued at home before stage 3 begins.)
8. Unwinding and closure	Affirm participants for having got so far on the programme. Are they now ready to move forward and see if they can sustain progress over the final Stage 3 part of the course?

Showing respect in my relationship

Think about the most important things you really want from your relationship. Can you put them in some sort of order below?

1.

2.

3.

4.

5.

6.

7.

8.

WHAT DO YOU NEED TO DO TO SHOW RESPECT WITHIN AND BUILD YOUR RELATIONSHIP?

Can you identify things that you can actually do that will demonstrate more respect?

- Listening with the intention of understanding your partner better?

- Watching out for the little things?

- Keeping commitments?

- Showing loyalty and trust?

- Apologising sincerely (but not just to talk your way out of something you've behaved yourself into)?

Preparing for Stage 3

Over the past 12 weeks you have explored the extent of your controlling and abusive behaviours within the following areas:

- Using physical violence
- Using threats and intimidation
- Being sexually disrespectful or abusive
- Bossing and controlling money
- Isolating and not supporting
- Being emotionally and verbally abusive.

You now need to continue to move away from behaviours which are forceful and negative and are to do with trying to keep some sort of power and control in your relationship. Whether in your current relationship, or if you move into a new relationship, you need to commit yourself to a mindset and a way of seeing things which is more about respect and equality in how you relate to your wife or partner. This will mean continuing to make actual changes in your behaviour and keeping these going. Think about the six positive areas of behaviour below and identify actual examples of how you hope to behave in such ways:

BEING NON-VIOLENT

I will…

BEING NON-THREATENING

I will…

BEING SEXUALLY RESPECTFUL

I will…

SHARING RESPONSIBILITY AND ECONOMIC PARTNERSHIP

I will…

TRUSTING AND SUPPORTING

I will…

RESPECTING

I will…

7

Stage 3: Maintaining the Change

Stage 3 is about consolidation and maintaining progress made. It is about facing up to the difficulties involved in sustaining positive change and coping with the reality of slip-up and relapse. Self-monitoring of progress in each of the six areas covered in Stage 2 is a central theme in this part of the programme, which takes place over several months. In addition several key areas are addressed:

- Relapse prevention
- Communication
- Arguments and conflict
- Belief system
- Lifestyle and stress management issues.
- Action planning for moving forward.

There is more time given at the start of each session than in Stage 2. This is to allow for the normal check-in, which continues on from Stage 2 and allows participants to refer to and reflect on their specific behaviours. An additional exercise is also introduced to participants. The 'Assessing my progress' exercise (below) is processed in each session as part of the check-in. It seeks to encourage participants to keep the positive change going and to be wary of the danger of relapse. It should help them to remain focused on how well they are staying on course in moving away from the abusive behaviours in the six key areas worked through in Stage 2. The exercise should help them to keep a clear vision of their destination and the way they can get there. That destination is behaviour within their relationships which is:

- non-violent
- non-threatening
- sexually intimate and caring
- fair and based on sharing and partnership
- trusting and supportive
- respectful.

Assessing my progress

You have been looking at six areas of behaviour on this programme. They are guidelines to the ways you should be thinking and acting if you are to have a more equal relationship with your partner. Think hard about each of the areas below. Score yourself from 1–5 for each area.

1 = making no progress   5 = making excellent progress

Comment on whether your work on the programme has helped you to be more honest and open as to the extent of your controlling behaviours, the difficulties you still experience, and also on how your children are finding things.

BEING NON-VIOLENT   **SCORE:**

Comments:

BEING NON-THREATENING   **SCORE:**

Comments:

BEING SEXUALLY RESPECTFUL   **SCORE:**

Comments:

SHARING RESPONSIBILITY, NEGOTIATION,   **SCORE:**
ECONOMIC PARTNERSHIP

Comments:

TRUSTING AND SUPPORTING   **SCORE:**

Comments:

RESPECTING   **SCORE:**

Comments:

Now give one example of how you are actually moving forward in one of the six positive areas of behaviour.

Stage 3 Session 1

Objectives of session

Participants will:

1. increase awareness of the difficult process of change and risk of relapse

2. assess their progress in moving towards more positive behaviour.

Outline of session

Content	Methods and process
1. Welcome and outlining of objectives	
2. Check-in	See guidelines, pp.124–25.
3. Maintaining positive change	Ask participants to think of the flight of an aeroplane. During the actual flight, wind, rain, turbulence, air traffic, human error and other factors all act on the plane. They move it slightly in different directions so that for most of the time the plane is not on the proper flight course. Briefly illustrate on flip chart.
	The point is that during a flight a pilot receives constant feedback from radar, ground control, other planes, etc. This lets him know that he is off-track and he can then make adjustments and get back on the right path. The absolutely crucial fact is that he knows where he is going so he can correct any mistakes.
	This is what this session is about. In Stage 2 the participants addressed six areas of behaviour in which they were seeking to think and act in more positive ways. They should begin to see this as their destination. This is where they are trying to get to. In each of the next six sessions they will be asked to assess how 'on track' they feel they are. (See 'Assessing my progress' form on p.169.) Participants to complete and share.

Stage 3 Session 1 (continued)

Content	Methods and process
4. Revisiting the change process	Remind participants of the Stages of Change process covered in Stage 1 Session 7. Re-emphasise the difficult nature of the process. Compare it with the stages that people go through when experiencing a crisis or trauma in their lives. (See 'Facing up to the difficult process of change' form on p.172.)
	Discuss in group. Can participants make any connections to their own experiences?
5. Cost–benefit analysis	Each participant to complete 'My decision balance sheet' (see p.173), considering the gains and losses of making changes in their behaviour.
	(It may help to do a general group balance sheet on the flipchart first and then each participant can do a personal one.)
6. Risk situations and lapse	The danger of slip-up and relapse back into old habits of controlling behaviour needs to be faced by participants. Is there also a risk that the old, more violent forms of behaviour could be replaced with more subtle behaviours in order to re-establish levels of dominance?
	Participants to complete 'Can you see it coming exercise?' and then process within the group.
7. Unwinding and closure	See guidelines, pp.125–26.

Facing up to the difficult process of change

DENIAL

I'm not responsible, it's out of my control, etc.

ANGER

It's her fault, this is doing my head in, etc.

BARGAINING

Look, it's not that bad. If I get a better job things will settle down; let's have a good holiday and sort it out together, etc.

DEPRESSION AND CONFUSION

There's no point, the harm's done, whatever **I do will be wrong, etc.**

ACCEPTANCE

It's my responsibility to do something about how I think and behave. I can't control the ways others will act or feel.

The above is a natural learning process; it may be a good sign that you are experiencing a range of negative feelings on the difficult journey to change.

(Adapted from Peck 1983)

My decision balance sheet

In any sort of change there will be gains and losses. You need to become aware of these in whatever you are trying to do. Deep down, do you really feel that you need to change? You may feel that you are losing control or that the plan will be too hard to stick to and you need to do something about your frustration building up. Put down as much as you can. Don't worry if you seem to be contradicting yourself as life is often like that. The important thing is to try hard to see how you view the situation at the moment.

Continue to be abusive – don't change		**Change my behaviour**	
Gains	*Losses*	*Gains*	*Losses*

Are most of your points in the central two columns?

(Adapted from Miller and Rollnick 1991)

Can you see it coming?

You may feel worried that you are going to behave in a violent and controlling way again. Can you tell the story of what you fear might happen and try to think of ways of avoiding violence?

What might happen?

When?

Where?

What mood might you be in?

If you carry out the above behaviour what will the effects be on:

- your wife/partner?

- your children?

- your wider family?

- others?

- yourself?

Stage 3 Session 2

Objectives of session

Participants will:

1. assess their progress in moving towards more positive behaviour

2. increase awareness of the importance of communication within relationships.

Outline of session

Content	Methods and process
1. Welcome and outlining of objectives	
2. Check-in and assessing progress	See guidelines, pp.124–25, and use form, p.169.
3. Communication between men and women	Refer participants back to session on manhood and masculinity (Stage 1 Session 4). Ask them to reflect on the differences in how boys and girls from about 7 years of age play and interact. During these important years until they become teenagers they tend to operate in two different worlds.
	Girls: Tend to play in smaller groups which minimise hostility and maximise co-operation. Tend to become better at managing and communicating their emotions and feelings. More vocal and keen to explore issues.
	Boys: Tend to play in larger groups, with more competition and attempts to dominate. Tend to play down emotions having to do with hurt, guilt, vulnerability, etc.; concentrate more on doing things than talking.
	How do such issues play out in later adult life in the differences between men and women, in how they see things, and in how they communicate?

Stage 3 Session 2 (continued)

Content	Methods and process
3. Communication between men and women (continued)	Brainstorm or work in small groups at identifying differences in how men and women communicate. Work through hand-out on 'Communication differences' (see p.177).
4. Exploring how we listen	Put the two statements from the 'Listening exercise' (see p.178) on the flip chart. Participants to write down how they feel they would respond.
	Process in terms of asking participants to reflect on their responses. Did they do any of the following:
	• *judging* – i.e. agreeing, disagreeing, criticising, blaming, etc.
	• *probing* – i.e. excessive, inappropriate questioning; interrupting
	• *advising* – i.e. jumping in with the solution and solving the problem
	• *interpreting* – i.e. trying to work it out, dismissing the person's concerns.
	These are not wrong in themselves but they may tend to block communication. They can 'close down' the other person and hinder her from sharing and exploring an important or difficult issue.
	Discuss and look for examples of listening which encourage the partner to develop issues. Can participants commit themselves to more *reflective listening*?
5. Listening to understand	Brainstorm positive consequences of positive listening.
	Stress to participants the absolute importance of being listened to within relationships. Next to physical survival, psychological survival is what most matters to us. Being listened to and feeling understood is the emotional and psychological equivalent of getting air – when you're gasping for the air of being understood nothing else matters!
	Despite the gender differences and the blocks to communication identified earlier in the session, can participants strive towards 'listening to understand?' Work through and discuss the hand-out below.
6. Unwinding and closure	See guidelines, p.126.

Communication differences between men and women

Men	Women
Tend to offer solutions to problems and want to achieve results	Tend to share feelings and discuss difficulties
Talk tends to revolve around passing on information and displaying knowledge, skill, status, and independence	Talk tends to revolve around sharing similar experiences, creating intimacy and rapport
Tend to mull things over, then come to the most correct, practical, and useful response	Tend to think aloud, share their inner dialogue, often use poetic licence to make their feelings known

- It is not clear whether these differences are because of how we are brought up or go deeper

- Everyone is different. These characteristics do not apply to everybody

- The important thing is to be AWARE of and TOLERATE the differences

- Can you go further and recognise the benefits of the differences?

(Adapted from Gray 1992)

Listening exercise

Ask participants to imagine they are at home with their partner.

You are lying on the settee watching TV. Imagine that your partner appears upset and annoyed and says each of the statements outlined below. What would your immediate response be on each occasion? Don't think about it too long, just write down as honestly as you can what you think you would say.

1. 'I'm fed up with how Ann's treating me at work. She's really doing my head in…'

2. 'The kids never tidy up the house. It's like a bomb hit it, it's a mess… all I bloody do is keep cleaning up after everyone.'

EXAMPLES OF POSSIBLE COMMUNICATION BLOCKS (SEE SESSION NOTES)

Statement 1

JUDGING:	You're too soft, you don't let me treat you like that…
PROBING:	Who are you seeing about it? What's she doing?
ADVISING:	Just ignore her, report her, give her worse back…
INTERPRETING:	She's maybe got problems, she's not getting enough…
Reflective listening:	She's really getting at you…?
	You're finding it tough to deal with her…?, etc.

Statement 2

JUDGING:	You're too soft, you let them get away with murder…
PROBING:	What exactly do they do when they come home?
ADVISING:	The moment they come in, get them organised…
INTERPRETING:	They probably are a bit stressed when they get home…
Reflective listening:	The state of the place is getting you down…?
	You're feeling fed up with the mess…?, etc.

It is important to stress that judgements, probing, advising and interpreting all have their place. However, they can sometimes act as roadblocks to communication and the underlying message may be:

'LISTEN TO ME; I KNOW BEST!'

(Adapted from Covey 1999)

Listening to understand

How well do you think you listen to your wife or partner? Do you often ignore, or can't be bothered, or pretend to listen, or listen to bits of what she says? Do you ever listen to try really to understand where she is coming from?

- The technique and skill in listening is just the tip of the iceberg. The great mass of the iceberg which you don't see is a deep and sincere desire to try to understand. In other words, you can do it if you really want to.

- Ninety per cent of an emotional message is non-verbal. You need to listen not only with your ears but with your eyes and heart. Listen for feelings.

- One of the best ways to learn to listen fully is simply to change the way you see your role as a listener – to see yourself as a 'faithful translator'. You have to work at it.

- If your wife or partner has lost trust in you because of what you have done in the past, you will need to be prepared to listen and to be sensitive to the situation.

Genuine listening will:

- give you valuable information about how your partner is feeling

- help you understand your partner's views and how they differ from yours

- show that you are concerned and taking your partner's concerns seriously.

Can you strive to listen so that you really understand your wife or partner and then seek to be understood yourself?

Stage 3 Session 3

Objectives of session

Participants will:

1. assess their progress in moving towards more positive behaviour

2. increase awareness of positive ways of handling conflict within relationships.

Outline of session

Content	Methods and process
1. Welcome and outlining of objectives	
2. Check-in and assessing progress	See guidelines, pp.124–25, and use form, p.169.
3. Exploring arguments and conflict	Conflict between couples can be built in, persistent and normal. Anger and its expression is a natural part of everybody's life. Remind participants of the techniques for managing anger in Stage 1 Session 2. It remains their responsibility to continue to manage their own anger. Even if their anger only comes out in negative ways on very rare occasions it will still affect the quality of all the rest of their lives. Their partners or children can *never* be sure when the raw nerve may be touched again.
	With this in mind this session is aimed at assisting participants to think about finding more positive ways to handle conflict in their lives. The first point is to recognise that conflict and differences within relationships can be tenacious and difficult.
	Brainstorm or work in small groups at identifying some of the difficulties.
	Work through 'Men and conflict in relationships' hand-out (see p.182).

Stage 3 Session 3 (continued)

Content	Methods and process
4. Understanding women's anger	Research has shown that one of the emotions girls are not encouraged to express is anger. How does this then play out in relationships where women have been subject to abusive behaviours? Participants to reflect on how safe it is for their partners to express their anger to them.
5. Conflict and children	Remind participants of the session which explored the effects of domestic violence on children. Point out that there has been some research carried out on the effects on children of conflict situations within families. Work through hand-out below and discuss issues to do with how children see conflict between their parents. Can participants identify with any of the findings and give examples?
6. Safer conflict	Work through the 'Exploring arguments' form on p.184. (Can do individually, in small groups or as brainstorm.) Take participants through the guidelines/ideas on the 'Safer conflict' hand-out on p.185 which may help in this difficult area. Discuss and look for positive examples.
7. Unwinding and closure	See guidelines, p.126.

Men and conflict in relationships

FEELING CORNERED BY AN ANGRY PARTNER

- Pulse rate increases

- Blood pressure goes up

- Testosterone surge

- Flooding with stress chemicals

- Feeling angry and on edge and waiting for the chance to retaliate

FIGHT	**FLIGHT**
Lash out	Withdraw
Go off like a fire cracker	Stonewall
	Repeated negative thoughts

CONFLICT IS DIFFICULT. IT MAY FEEL LIKE IT IS SORTED OUT, AND THEN IT MAY TEAR YOU APART AGAIN.

BUT REMEMBER:

IT IS NOT HEALTHY TO KEEP AVOIDING DISAGREEMENT OR CONFLICT – BUT THE USE OF VIOLENCE IS NEVER JUSTIFIED.

Children and conflict

Anger and conflict in themselves do not do harm to children. It is how they are handled that may affect them.

CONFLICT AND ANGER EXPRESSION FROM THE CHILD'S IMMEDIATE PERSPECTIVE

Physical anger expression is not only the most distressing form of anger expression, it has also been most clearly and consistently linked with the later development of *mental health problems.*

Children tend not to respond in a negative way to arguments and fights if they see that they have been resolved (apology, compromise).

Children tend to respond in a moderately negative way to arguments and fights if they have been partially sorted out (topic changed, submission of one side).

Children tend to respond in a highly negative way to unresolved arguments or fights (continued open fighting, silent treatment).

CHILDREN PERCEIVE AS POSITIVE ANY PROGRESS TOWARDS RESOLUTION.

(Adapted from Cummings and Davies 1994)

Exploring arguments

What makes an argument abusive rather than productive?

What rules might help to keep an argument non-abusive?

What are the gains and losses from arguing abusively?

Gains:

Losses:

What are the gains and losses from arguing non-abusively?

Gains:

Losses:

Safer conflict

Always remember that it is not the difficulties and problems in themselves which destroy a relationship. Every couple struggles with how to discipline children, how to handle money issues, the sexual side of their relationship, etc. It is *how* a couple discuss such sore points that matters most for the fate of their relationship.

WHEN IN AN ARGUMENT

- Try to stick to one topic and allow partner to state her view
- Show that you are listening. Don't ignore, put down, react as if being attacked; try to ignore the nasty words in order to hear the message
- Try to keep down tension (work at calming-down relaxation techniques, etc.). Find ways to get your stress levels to wear off if you have got worked up
- Challenge your own thinking. Where are you coming from? Why does your partner's anger cause you to be so upset in the first place?
- Plumb your own feelings
- Never fight physically
- Try to see it from your partner's perspective. Maybe she is trying to sort out something that will help to keep your relationship more healthy
- Take responsibility if you have acted wrongly.

Remember that these are very hard to put into practice. Your experience from early childhood and your immediate instinct and strong gut feeling will be to go with your anger and hurt. You have to over-learn these techniques. Practise them in less stressful situations before having to use them in the heat of the moment.

WHATEVER YOU DO, YOU HAVE TO REACH AN AGREEMENT WITH YOUR PARTNER ABOUT HOW TO DISAGREE!

(Adapted from Goldman 1996)

Stage 3 Session 4

Objectives of session

Participants will:

1. assess their progress in moving towards more positive behaviour

2. identify positive changes in their beliefs and mindsets about women and relationships.

Outline of session

Content	Methods and process
1. Welcome and outlining of objectives	
2. Check-in and assessing progress	See guidelines, pp.124–25; and use form on p.169.
3. Handling disagreement	Following on from the last session, participants to complete and share exercise below on how they are trying to deal with issues in which there is clear disagreement between themselves and their partners. Process within the group.
4. Thinking about mindsets	Begin with an analogy of participants being lost in a large city. He has with him the map of another city! He adopts a very positive attitude and tries really hard. However, with the wrong map, no matter how he behaves or how positive his attitude he will still be lost! He needs the right map. Inform participants that one authority in the area of domestic violence has identified three critical beliefs as being present in a large number of men who use controling and abusive behaviour against their partners. These beliefs are the map that such men use. It is the wrong map but many men are stuck with it. They need to change this map. Participants to work at exercise 'Exploring my belief system' (see p.189) and honestly explore where they see themselves in relation to such key beliefs about men and women and their expectations about respective roles.

Stage 3 Session 4 (continued)

Content	Methods and process
4. Thinking about mindsets (continued)	Discuss within group. Can participants give examples of when, however subtly, they related to the beliefs on the 'abusive' side of the continuum? Are there still some aspects of such beliefs about? Can they identify how and when they started to shift their beliefs and move their mindset?
	Emphasise the critical importance of this exercise. The programme rests on an idea that it is the way we see the world and our ideas which will ultimately help us explain and understand our behaviour. Participants should be able to make some sort of connection between the abusive behaviours they listed in Stage 1 Session 2, and the ideas in the exercise. In one sense they should have a set of negative ideas and beliefs of which they have become more aware, and have put on the table; they are now moving away from these and towards a more positive mindset – a new map which is more appropriate for positive relationships.
5. Moving forward	Participants to complete exercise and discuss in group (see p.190). Each person to select what has been a significant area of movement for himself and also an area that he needs to continue to work on.
6. Unwinding and closure	See guidelines, p.126.

Handling disagreement

You have admitted a problem with your abusive and controlling behaviour; you have accepted responsibility for it and have worked at in on this programme. Now reflect on the difficult issues below and as honestly as possible state how you deal with them.

Your partner asks you to do something that she feels very strongly about but you definitely do not want to do it.

Your partner refuses your request for something that you really want.

Exploring my belief system

WHERE ARE YOU ON THE CONTINUUM?

| ABUSIVE BELIEFS HELD BY MEN WHO USE CONTROLLING AND VIOLENT BEHAVIOURS WITHIN RELATIONSHIPS | | POSITIVE BELIEFS HELD BY NON-ABUSING MEN |

The wrong map   **The right map**

Basically men are superior   1   2   3   4   5   Men and women
to women   are equal
WHY?

Men should remain   1   2   3   4   5   Men should be
separate and detached   committed and
from the relationship   part of the relationship
WHY?

Men should be cared   1   2   3   4   5   Men and women
for and nurtured by their   should support
partners   and care for each other
WHY?

(Adapted from Russell 1995)

Are you moving forward positively?

Think about the following list and select those that you have done recently. If you are doing the things on this list it is a sign that you are becoming less controlling. Briefly write what you did and when.

- Realised I was angry and did something to calm myself down

- Admitted to someone that I was wrong about something

- Gave way over an issue I was arguing about which I felt was important

- Accepted my partner (ex-partner) doing something for herself

- Listened to my partner without interrupting or contradicting her

- Told my partner she was looking well when I was not trying to get something

- Asked my partner's opinion before making arrangements for both of us

- Took my full share of responsibility

- Consulted my partner before making a financial decision

Stage 3 Session 5

Objectives of session

Participants will:

1.   assess their progress in moving towards more positive behaviour

2.   identify positive changes they can make in their lifestyles.

Outline of session

Content	Methods and process
1. Welcome and outlining of objectives	
2. Check-in and assessing progress	See guidelines, pp.124–25, and use form on p.169.
3. Balanced lifestyle	For each of us and for our relationships and families, it is important to think about the four key areas of our lives. These are: THE PHYSICAL THE SOCIAL THE MENTAL THE SPIRITUAL. Take participants through the ideas below and ask them to reflect on their situation within each of the main areas. Do they need to address any issues?
4. Lifestyle issues	Each person is responsible for his behaviours and needs to address them fully and honestly if he is to move forward. However, lifestyle issues are important, particularly in ways that may either hinder or support behaviour change. The purpose of this session is to encourage participants to reflect on a range of lifestyle issues relevant to their own situation. Each participant to work on 'Positive life trends' form (below) and feedback to group. Brief discussion.
5. Managing stress	Group to carry out a brief audit of the stress they are experiencing (see p.194). Work through stress management exercise on pp.195–96.
6. Unwinding and closure	See guidelines, p.126.

Balanced Lifestyle

PHYSICAL

Exercise, physical activity, healthy diet and managing stress.

SOCIAL

Building relationships, deepening friendships, giving service, listening with understanding, co-operating with others.

MENTAL

Reading, planning and developing talents, learning new skills.

SPIRITUAL

Meditating, having values and principles, praying, spiritual practices, etc.

(Adapted from Covey 1992)

Think about how you have actually spent your life over the past fortnight. How many of the above positive activities were you able to commit yourself to?

To what extent is your life dominated by the struggle to make a living, to achieve, to suceed?

Are you spending some of your time doing things that are of no use or indeed harmful to yourself?

Positive life trends

Think of things in your life that are helping you to be 'on the up'. Put each one on the stairs below:

5_____

4_____

3_____

2_____

1_____

GOING DOWNHILL?

What are the things pulling you down?

1_____

2_____

3_____

4_____

5_____

Is there anything you can do to help you get more on the up?

1.

2.

What causes stress?

Consider the following list. Stress management consultants have indicated that if you clock up a score of more than 150 points for events within the last year, the chances are that you will experience a downturn in health of some kind. A score over 300 will almost certainly lead to major health problems unless action is taken.

Death of spouse	100	New boss	28
Divorce	75	Children leaving home	27
Marital separation	65	Problems with in-laws	26
Prison sentence	65	Winning award	26
Death of someone close in the family	65	Partner changing type of work	25
Serious injury or illness	55	Beginning or stopping business course	23
Getting married	50	Change in living conditions	23
Redundancy or dismissal	48	Change in personal habits	22
Marital reconciliation	45	Falling out with boss	21
Retirement	44	Change in working conditions	20
Illness affecting close family member	44	Moving house	20
Pregnancy	40	Children changing school	19
Sexual difficulties	40	Change in social activities	18
New baby	39	Change in religious activities	18
Change in business	38	Taking out loan	17
Change in financial affairs	38	Altered sleeping habits	17
Death of a close friend	38	Change in family location	16
Change in work	37	Dieting	15
Change in relationship with your partner	36	Holidays	15
Mortgage rate rise	31	Christmas	15
Loss of mortgage	30	Minor law-breaking	15

(Adapted from Craze 1998)

Introduction to stress management

RELAX THE BODY, CALM THE MIND

This relaxation technique is very simple, but effective. It is best to do the exercise on the floor but it can be practised in a chair. Playing soft relaxation music in the background can be helpful to this session.

1. Sit or lie down quietly with the back straight and the arms alongside the body.

2. Allow the body to settle with feet apart, and the palms of the hand turned up to the ceiling with the fingers gently curled.

3. Keeping the mouth closed, breathe slowly through the nose. Allow the stomach to rise on the inhalation and fall on the exhalation. Concentrate on establishing this slow, relaxed breathing pattern for about five minutes.

4. To relax the muscles:

- Tense the whole of the right foot, release and let go
- Tense the whole of the right leg, release and let go
- Tense the whole of the left foot, release and let go
- Tense the whole of the left leg, release and let go
- Clench the right fist as tight as you can, release and let go
- Tense the whole of the right arm, release and let go
- Clench the left fist as tight as you can, release and let go
- Tense the whole of the left arm, release and let go
- Tense the shoulders by bringing them up towards the ears, hold the tension, release and let go, bringing the shoulders well down
- Tense the head and face by tightening the forehead, closing the eyes tightly and clenching the teeth. Then release and let go all tension out of the face and head and have the teeth slightly apart
- Feel all tension draining from the body. If you are aware of tension in any part of the body, release it and let it go.

Introduction to stress management (continued)

5.   Take your awareness back to the breathing and become aware of any changes in the breathing pattern.

6.   If any thoughts are rising, do not try to stop or judge them; acknowledge them, then let them go.

7.   Allow the body to enjoy this state of relaxation.

8.   Enjoy the stillness of the mind, the calmness of the body.

9.   When the relaxation is completed, stretch the arms up and over the head and the legs and feet away from the body.

10.   Stand up slowly, and let the arms hang alongside the body.

Each participant needs to consider his own situation and lifestyle circumstances when deciding whether he needs to build this or other leisure activities into his life.

Stage 3 Session 6

Objectives of session

Participants will:

1. assess their progress in moving towards more positive behaviour

2. plan to make and sustain positive change.

Outline of session

Content	Methods and process
1. Welcome and outlining of objectives	
2. Check-in and assessing progress	See guidelines, pp.124–25 and use form on p.169.
3. Dealing with the end of relationships	As a result of their past behaviour some of the participants' relationships may not have survived or their future may remain uncertain. Discuss points on hand-out on p.198 for men no longer in their relationship. Other men could reflect on how they would handle separation or the end of their relationship.
4. Action planning and moving forward	Read out visualisation exercise to participants. This can be a powerful exercise. Take time to check out how individual participants are feeling. Remind them of the aeroplane and how easy it is to go off-track. None of us are perfect. We have all done things we regret. However, we can change. We can seek to strive for positive goals in our lives. It is never too late. But we need an idea of where we want to go: a map and a plan for our destination. Each participant to complete his individual 'Positive change' sheet (see p.200). Use 'long-term solutions' form (below) as prompter for participants to identify specific strategies in their continuing efforts to change.
5. Evaluation	Remind participants of their agreement to participate in evaluation of the programme. Inform them of particular arrangements that are to be made to carry this out. (See Chapter 9.)
6. Affirmation and closure	Affirm the commitment and determination that participants have shown in getting to the end of the programme. Allow a little more time for final closure and for participants to share their feelings about the ending of the programme.

Dealing with the end
of a relationship

It may be that your relationship has not survived or its future is uncertain. This is a very difficult situation that you need to face with care and sensitivity. Are you able to move through it in as positive a way as possible? Consider the following issues:

- Do you feel that you are in any way harassing your ex-partner?

- Are you able *not* to say negative things about her to your children or your family?

- Are you experiencing any obsessive thoughts about her?

- Are you able to get on with your life?

- Have you examined in general your negative thoughts and feelings towards women?

What do you really want in life?

Participants are asked to relax, settle back to listen and to think about what is about to be said. It may help to shut their eyes and to try just to go with the exercise.

Then read out the following:

> You have worked over the last eight or nine months at trying to move away from using violent and controlling behaviour in your relationship. You now need to think how you intend to go forward.
>
> What do you really want in your life with your wife or partner and children? Can you go forward and face the challenges of your life, the setbacks, the tensions, and know that violence and fear will not be a part of it?
>
> Think deeply. Imagine it is three years into the future, and you are sitting once again in this room. Your partner, one of your children and someone you know are going to describe how they have found the three years since you finished the programme. First your wife or partner will speak:
>
> What would you like her to say about you?
> What kind of husband or partner would you like her to describe?
> What difference would you like to have made in her life?
>
> Then one of your children will speak: What would you like him or her to say?
>
> Then a friend?
>
> It is in your hands as to how you are going to move forward from this programme.

Can you look further into the future? What would you like to write in your obituary? This will help you see what you really want to live for!

Always remember and continually remind yourself that the most common deathbed regrets relate to neglected relationships, not unfinished business!

Now before we move on, just take a few moments to quickly jot down your impressions from this exercise.

(Adapted from Covey 1992 and Hardiman 2000)

Plan for positive change

What is the most important change I have made as a result of this programme?

What other changes have I made and do I need to continue making? (See 'Long-term solutions' sheet)

The most important reasons why I want to make these changes are:

The steps I am taking in changing are:

The ways other people can help me are:

People   **Possible ways to help**

Some things that could interfere:

I know that my plan is working if:

Long-term solutions

Think about the following list and select those that you feel are most important to use as part of your action plan for the future:

- Consistently take full responsibility for my violence
- Give my partner space and time to decide what she wants at her own pace
- Avoid side-tracking, minimizing or blaming my partner
- Not rushing my partner or giving her ultimatums or deadlines
- Stop feeling sorry for myself, focus on my own goals for self-change
- Maintain a positive attitude about my situation
- Actively listen to my partner, let her express her feelings
- Focus on my own problems
- Avoid any accusations or criticisms of my partner no matter how strongly I feel them
- Develop my self-care plan
- Don't expect instant results
- Stay off alcohol or drugs
- Get support to help me with staying sober
- Stop trying to control my partner's thoughts or feelings
- Learn more about how my violence has affected my children
- Recognise my shortcomings as a father but try to do better
- Learn to accept uncomfortable feelings, without resorting to violence, or self-destructive behaviour
- Practise positive self-talk.

IF SEPARATED

- Respect my partner's wishes about the amount of contact she wants to have with me
- Don't pressure her for more contact
- Don't attempt to make her feel guilty about my situation, being out of the house, not being able to see the children as much as I want, not knowing where I stand with her, etc.
- Make the best of whatever contact I have with my partner or children.

8

Programme Integrity and Evaluation

The objectives for participants completing the PVR programme are:

- Increase understanding of their use of controlling and abusive behaviour against their wife or partner

- Increase understanding of the effects of this behaviour

- Take full responsibility for their use of this behaviour

- Change their behaviour so that they do not use violence against women and children.

The key issue of just how effective the PVR programme is in achieving these objectives is the focus of this chapter. The first step is to make sure that the programme is delivered in the way outlined in this manual, in other words that there is programme integrity reflected in well-designed, managed and facilitated programmes.

Tight Design

The content and design of the programme, its underpinning value-base as well as its knowledge and skill requirements, are set out in this book. It is targeted at men who feel they have a problem with their use of violent and controlling behaviours within their relationships. The rationale of the programme is to assist such men in a difficult process of moving towards more positive, egalitarian and respectful behaviours within their relationships. Each session is clearly structured to move participants through a process of learning and change. Clear tasks within each session are aligned to meet defined objectives which come together to meet the goals of each of the three stages, and, it is hoped, the overall objectives outlined above.

Sound Management

It will clearly be the responsibility of agencies who wish to use the PVR programme to ensure that the organisational culture and structure is in tune with what is required. Agencies will need to recognise fully the commitment involved, and take the appropriate steps to ensure that they do the following:

- Understand the PVR programme and promote it properly
- Monitor its delivery
- Evaluate and improve delivery if required
- Procure appropriate funds, equipment and accommodation
- Support facilitators
- Manage information around the programme
- Build partnership and consultancy arrangements with other agencies, particularly Women's Aid, to ensure that their perspective is prominent.

Skilled Practitioners

Key issues for facilitators that are critical to maintaining the integrity of the programme include:

- commitment to the values of the programme
- an awareness of the causes, extent and effects of male domestic violence against females
- a clear understanding of the contents of all the sessions
- delivery as outlined in this manual
- maintenance of positive working environment
- being comfortable with adapting an adult learning model and with seeking to understand the process of change and maintaining the motivation of participants
- having an understanding of the cognitive-behavioural approach
- taking time to plan, prepare and debrief
- monitoring and evaluating the programme and its delivery.

This manual contains a sufficient basis of material to allow a committed worker to operate effectively in this area. As outlined in Chapter 3, considerable patience, skill and support will be required. However, it is important to remember that this is primarily an awareness-raising adult education course layered with a cognitive-behavioural approach. It is specifically targeted at men who are already acknowledging that they have a problem and are prepared to address it. It is about providing space and a meaningful opportunity for men to do this. As stated earlier, with commitment to the approach, and the systems outlined in this chapter in place, this type of intervention can be delivered by a wide range of people. Supportive supervision or co-working arrangements with someone with more experience in this area may assist prospective facilitators to increase their confidence and competence.

Evaluation Issues

The key question is whether or not the PVR programme can be effective in helping or persuading men to change their unacceptable behaviours and attitudes. To what extent can the objectives outlined at the beginning of this chapter be achieved? At this stage we have to try to go forward without definite answers to such questions. There is some research into criminal justice based programmes which would suggest that men can learn to change their violent behaviour, question key supporting attitudes and become the regulators of their own behaviour (Dobash *et al.* 1996). Of course we are not comparing like with like and it is imperative that evaluation is built into PVR and similar programmes as they develop. 'Numerous ingenious programmes have been carefully nurtured into existence and steered through to their conclusions, only to disappear – because not one shred of evidence had been gathered about their clientele, their functioning or their effectiveness' (Maguire 1995, p.50).

It is only through the gathering of detailed information and feedback from participants and more importantly, the views of wives and partners, that we may begin to establish whether or not the programme is associated with desistance from, or continuation of violent, abusive or controlling behaviours. It is critical that there is an 'in-built continuing and rigorous evaluation that gives abused women a voice, particularly in defining and measuring positive outcomes' (Mullender 1996, p.247). This can be facilitated through an initial contact and the offer of an information session to partners at the beginning of the programme. At this meeting the issue of their involvement in providing confidential and independently gathered feedback on what they feel about the programme can be discussed. This can be carried out at the end of the programme and then again at agreed intervals afterwards to establish if there are long-term benefits from the programme. (I have provided suggested interview schedules for collecting and recording such information.)

Getting independent research carried out is expensive, and the possibility of negotiating local arrangements with academic institutions or with community development or crime prevention schemes needs to be explored. In the short term, it should be relatively straightforward to obtain some data on whether or not there are positive outcomes playing out in the lives of participants and their partners and families (see interview schedules). The key point is to build in an independent element to the gathering of such information. I would also recommend that such material is made as widely available as possible. This can be done through the Internet and also through social work and other journals. This is important for three reasons:

- It will provide a form of quality assurance in that it will lead to critical scrutiny and feedback from others interested in this area of work

- It may assist others to benefit in terms of developing their own practice initiatives

- It will assist in the ongoing process of theory building and the development of a body of empirical knowledge.

(Chapman and Hough 1998)

If there are early positive indicators, then it may be possible to carry out more systematic research. This can begin to look at how the process of intervention actually helps effect change. For example, are there key inputs, is there an essential length of course, how helpful is the first stage just as a general awareness-raising programme for all young men, etc?

PVR is in its infancy. Whether it has a future will depend on the gathering of evidence which shows that for some men, their wives, partners and families, it can actually assist in a process which leads to the achievement of the positive objectives outlined at the beginning of the chapter.

Evaluation (Participants)

Reason(s) for doing course:

Number of sessions attended:

Reason(s) for missing sessions:

Was the programme (underline):

(a) Too long   About the right length   Too short

(b) Better than expected   Just as you expected   Worse than expected

(c) Too hurried   About the right pace   Too slow

1.   How helpful has the programme been in increasing your understanding of your use of controlling and abusive behaviour against your partner?

        6   5   4   3   2   1

     very helpful   not helpful

WHY?

2.   How helpful has the programme been in increasing your awareness of the negative effects of such behaviour?

        6   5   4   3   2   1

     very helpful   not helpful

WHY?

Evaluation (Participants) (Continued)

3.   How helpful was the programme in enabling you to take full responsibility for your behaviour?

        6   5   4   3   2   1

    very helpful   not helpful

WHY?

4.   How helpful was the programme in helping you to move away from such behaviour and towards positive change?

        6   5   4   3   2   1

    very helpful   not helpful

WHY?

5.   How helpful do you feel the programme has been in helping you not to use violent or controlling behaviour against your partner or children in the future?

        6   5   4   3   2   1

    very helpful   not helpful

WHY?

What were the least helpful parts of the programme?

How would you describe the course to a friend who was worried about his behaviour with his partner?

Evaluation (Partners)

Your (ex)partner or (ex)husband has recently completed the PVR programme. This is an opportunity for you to give your opinion of the course and any other points you wish to make. This will be confidential.

Date of completion of programme:

1.   Have you noticed any change in the following areas?

His attitudes

To you:

Your children:

Your extended family:

His behaviour:

To you:

Your children:

Your extended family:

Evaluation (Partners) (continued)

2.   Have there been any occasions of physical violence since he commenced the course?

3.   Have there been any incidents of emotional, verbal, or threatening behaviour since he has been on the programme?

          How much, and is it getting better or worse?

4.   To what extent are you in fear of him?

	6	5	4	3	2	1

extremely fearful   not at all
fearful

WHY?

5.   Has he shared with you what he does on the programme?

          If not, do you think he should?

WHY?

Evaluation (Partners) (continued)

6.   Would you recommend the programme to a close friend who was having difficulty with her partner's behaviour?

WHY?

7.   Did you attend the Partner Information Session?

WHY?

Did you find it useful?

WHY?

Did you take up any of the services offered to you at that session?

WHY?

8.   Any other comments you would like to make about the programme?

Thank you for your time in providing the above information, which will be treated confidentially. It will be very important in the continuing development of the programme.

9

Conclusion and the Way Forward

The behaviour of men has been viewed by some as a rolling male disaster, increasingly out of control with unforeseen consequences for the future. In one sense this publication is acknowledging the seriousness of the situation. However, there are also encouraging signs. The women's movement has acted as a positive current for change and has assisted in highlighting the need for a range of changes with regard to reducing levels of violence, and these are ongoing. In addition, many men can and do play positive roles in the lives of their families and this is happening within committed relationships based on equality. This programme is not about watering down the male role, or about trying to create SNAGs (sensitive new age guys) (Biddulph 1999). The motto for European Year of Prevention of Violence against Women is *Real men do not abuse women*. The vision remains one of reducing the use of violent behaviour within relationships. It is about striving to advance both genders together.

To this end the PVR programme is aimed at providing a unique opportunity for men to step back and work at issues for which they have a responsibility. Are they able to take ownership of their behaviour and the self-deceptions and distortions that have accompanied it? Are they able to orientate themselves to living more positively within relationships? Can they move towards creating more respectful positive relationships with their wives and children?

The sessions outlined in this manual have been piloted during 1999. As indicated in the last chapter, it is much too early to draw definitive conclusions and there remains a need for ongoing, thorough and independent evaluation. Nevertheless, some information has emerged over the past 12 months. This has been gleaned from several sources:

1. Contributions from men during sessions of the programme

2. Feedback from men during and after completion of the programme

3. Feedback from wives and partners

4. Feedback from counsellors working with couples.

A Model for Positive Change

It has been possible to make links between this information and a model of possible positive change. This model has emerged from research into the progress of men taking part in criminal justice based programmes (Dobash *et al.* 1996). The names John and Ann are used for a number of men and their partners who engaged in the programme. The statements below are taken directly from the feedback of the four sources listed above.

TO RECOGNISE THAT IT IS POSSIBLE FOR THEM TO CHANGE

'I used to think that these things just happened and I couldn't do anything about it. It's down to me now to stop.'

'Saying a leopard can't change its spots is just an excuse.'

TO SEE THE NEED TO MAKE CHANGES TO SOME ASPECTS OF THEIR BEHAVIOUR

'I just sat back and let Ann worry about all the money stuff, I didn't care as long as we had enough money. If we didn't then I would get on to her. I know I was opting out. I have to get more involved.'

'I would just have a long face for days, keeping it in. Ann knew there was something wrong, but she didn't know what and was afraid to ask.'

'He understands more what he was doing to me.'

TO BECOME CLEARER AS TO THE IMPORTANT REASONS FOR CHANGING

'We have the baby now, I don't want her to grow up and somebody doing to her what I've done to her mother. I have to sort this out.'

'What sort of relationship is it if Ann is afraid of me?'

TO SEE THE BEHAVIOUR THEY USE AS SOMETHING THEY DECIDE TO USE; THEY ARE THE SUBJECT, NOT THE OBJECT

'I used to blame Ann. OK, she still does my head in sometimes but I know now that if I become aggressive that is my decision and not hers.'

'I remember one time Ann was going through a really bad time but I was so caught up in an urgent job I wouldn't listen to her. She kept interrupting and disrupting my work. I lost it and slapped her. I always thought it was her fault. Now I can see that I decided to give her a good slap, just one, to give her a message. It was really deliberate!'

TO MOVE TOWARDS BETTER INTERNAL CONTROLS OF THEIR BEHAVIOUR

'I know it's up to me. I can recognise some of my early warning signs and talk about them.'

'I still know if he's not happy about something, but we can talk it out more. He will listen to my side more.'

'I have been really angry with him. He stayed calmer than before. He is starting to accept that maybe we should separate.'

TO SHIFT THEIR MINDSET WITH REGARD TO THEIR THOUGHTS AND EMOTIONS

'I never thought there would be so much arguing in a relationship. I know it must be something to do with how I expect Ann to be because I never lose it at work.'

'I always thought I had to stay in control or she would walk all over me.'

TO COMMIT THEMSELVES TO CHANGES THROUGH TALKING, LISTENING, LEARNING AND THINKING

'I can say things here that I don't say to anyone else. It really helps me to talk and think about these things. I've learnt a lot.'

'There is so much I have to do to try to keep the change going.'

'I could be a friend to John now for the sake of the child – but I could never take him back.'

TO IDENTIFY SPECIFIC ELEMENTS OF CHANGE IN BOTH BEHAVIOUR AND ATTITUDES

'When I'm annoyed at home now, I don't go quiet and keep it all in and then explode. I make the effort to communicate now. In the past I didn't bother.'

'It's taken me a long time to realise that I am jealous and I am still keeping an eye on things. I don't have that right.'

Of course it is impossible to say how meaningful and long-lasting such changes will be. As one woman put it to me, 'I know in my head that he has changed but in my heart I'm not sure.' For some women the fear may remain. It is also the case that several participants have commenced the programme and then failed to sustain their commitment. There will remain those for whom positive change is difficult. They will still be prepared to use violence or the threat of it. However, even in the case of those men who left the programme early, it was still possible to give information to wives and partners and to encourage links to Women's Aid. Perhaps this may play out positively for such women in that they will not tolerate further abusive behaviour. They may be now more prepared to use the criminal justice system if the violence continues, rather than to continue to hope for change.

Domestic violence is pervasive and embedded within our communities. In one sense, it is a public health issue which requires a range of preventative responses as well as strong societal sanctions. If preventative educational courses such as PVR are confined to the criminal justice system, only a small minority of men who employ violence will be reached. More widely available programmes may assist even a small number of men to move through the difficult change process outlined above. They may have a positive impact and reduce the level of violence and fear in the lives of just a few women and children. For these reasons alone they are worth while. Moreover, they may go further. Educational programmes will promote positive messages about respectful behaviours within relationships and will ripple out into the community. They may act as a focus for action against men's violence, and offer new innovative approaches to such a social crisis.

This manual began with a reference to the ongoing peace process within Northern Ireland. John Hume has struggled for many years against the use of political violence. He has highlighted the importance of continually working to change the language and ideas of those who may use such violence. He has sought to promote a message of peaceful conflict-resolution: 'I say it and go on saying it until I hear the man in the pub saying my words back to me' (Hume in Routledge 1997, p.5). The PVR programme is presented as one way of helping men who may use domestic violence to learn and develop new mindsets, and language which is about moving away from the use of violence within their relationships.

APPENDIX I

Information Session

This is optional but is recommended as a way of getting information and a feel of the course to groups of men who may be thinking about the need to address some of their own behaviours. It is usually an 'open' session. Any man who may be interested can come along without any cost or commitment, just to find out more about the programme. The session focuses on the principles underpinning the programme, the contract, the nature and style of the work. A suggested outline is included. The session is not essential, as some participants may have made direct approaches and discussed the course individually and in detail. They may have then contracted to commence the programme.

Information Session

Objectives of session

Participants will:

1. learn about the contract, content and style of the PVR programme

2. be able to ask questions about the above.

Outline of session

Content	Methods and Process
1. Welcome	Affirm men for their decision to come along and listen to what is on offer. Outline the objectives to them. Indicate at this point that there is no need for introductions. This is an opportunity for them to find out about the programme in order to help them decide whether it is relevant to them. Point out to men that there is a fair amount of information to cover, but that time will be left at the end for any questions they may have.
2. Why are you here?	Go through Figure Appendix 1.1. Leave it to participants to come up with their own answers.
3. PVR programme principles	Work through principles in Figure Appendix 1.2.
4. Content and style of programme	Emphasise that the PVR course is firmly based on assisting men to explore in great detail their use of controlling and violent behaviours against their wives or partners. Through increasing their understanding of the effects of such behaviour and awareness of the reasons why they use it, the programme will seek to support them in a process of positive change.

Information Session (continued)

Content	Methods and Process
4. Content and style of programme (continued)	It will offer a unique opportunity to participants to have time and space really to think about and work at their behaviour.
	It is an *adult education and learning course*, not counselling!
	It involves taking part in listening to information, working individually at issues, and in various group exercises and discussions.
	It is about CHANGE!
	Use the 'Is change possible' hand-out on p.112.
5. Programme contract	Stress to prospective participants that they need to know clearly what they are getting into so that they can make an informed decision. Work though each of the points in the PVR contract (see p.222).
6. Opportunity for questions	Encourage participants to raise any issues and concerns that they may have, and respond.
7. Registration arrangements	Inform participants of the procedures for registration and provide details on times and location of next programme.

Why are you here ?

* Have you ever been violent or aggressive to your partner?

* Have you ever lost control?

* Have you ever regretted the abusive way you've been with your partner?

* Are you worried that you may do something that could cause physical or emotional harm to your partner?

* Are you worried about the effects of your behaviour on your children or family?

Appendix 1.1. Why are you here?

Principles of the PVR programme

✸ Protection and safety of women

✸ Zero tolerance of domestic violence

✸ Responsibility for own behaviour

✸ Change is possible

✸ A positive, research-based programme open to all sections of the community

Appendix 1.2. Principles of PVR programme.

PVR programme contract

PVR is a preventative educational programme for men who feel they have a problem with their use of violent and controlling behaviours in their relationships. Participation on the programme **CANNOT** be used to avoid being held accountable for **ANY** acts of criminal behaviour.

I declare that:

- I will not use physical violence against my partner/ex-partner while I am taking part in the PVR course.

- I am not currently facing or likely to be facing any criminal charges for violence or breaches of personal protection, exclusion or non-molestation orders against my present or former partner.

- I understand that PVR is providing an educational service for me and will not be offering medical or psychological diagnosis, treatment or counselling services.

- I will attend all sessions on time in an alcohol- and drug-free state.

- I agree to maintain the confidentiality of the group and not share personal information about my partner or ex-partner.

- I understand that my partner will receive information regarding the content and aims of the PVR programme. She will be invited to a separate information session about the programme and will be advised of a range of services available for her protection, including Belfast Women's Aid and the Help Line.

- I will treat all other members of the group and the facilitators with respect.

- I agree to some of the sessions being observed by another party. (This is to ensure that the programme is being delivered appropriately.)

- I understand that if there are child protection issues that are of concern, these will have to be reported to the relevant agencies.

- I understand that if I disclose specific details of a serious criminal offence, this information may be passed on to the police.

- I accept that PVR will not provide reports for court.

- I have read, fully understand and agree to abide by all the above conditions.

Signed: _____

Date: _____

Use of Role Play

The option of playing out in role some of the example scenarios or participants' own reported behaviours exists at various points in the programme. The following points are offered to facilitators who feel confident and competent in using such methods.

- First, initial resistance to role play is common but with humour and gentle persuasion it can be overcome

- Having said the above, no one should feel obliged to participate and should be able to withdraw if they wish

- Persons should not play themselves in role

- Use fictitious names for the role play

- Use separate chairs not used by participants for the exercise

- Give basic script to each character but do not over-define. The main aim will be usually just to illustrate and demonstrate a particular controlling behaviour and how it impacts

- Agree with group to use 'freeze' to stop role play, with participants staying still to illustrate non-verbal threatening behaviours; or it may also be possible to suggest and then practise alternative non-violent behaviours

- If anyone gets upset during a role play, give attention

- It is important to de-role in a clear way, almost to make it a ritual:

    Get participants to share how they are feeling in role
    Ask them to leave their role, return to their own seats and say who they are
    Ask if they are comfortable with being themselves again

- Stress that participants are given permission within role to act abusively, although that is not the way they behave normally within the group

- Make sure everyone is OK.

References

Adams, D. (1988) 'Treatment models of men who batter: a profeminist analysis.' In K. Yllo and M. Bograd (eds) *Feminist Perspectives on Wife Abuse*. Beverly Hills: Sage.

Archer, J. (ed) (1994) *Male Violence*. London: Routledge.

Bancroft, L. (1997) 'Batterers' intervention programmes – do they work?' *Family Law*. February.

Bandura, A. (1973) *Aggression: A Social Learning Analysis*. Englewood Cliffs, NJ: Prentice Hall.

Bandura, A. (1986) *Social Foundation of Thoughts and Actions: A Cognitive Theory*. Englewood Cliffs, NJ: Prentice Hall.

Benson, J.F. (1996) *Working More Creatively with Groups*. London: Routledge.

Biddulph, S. (1999) *Manhood*. Stroud: Hawthorn Press.

Bowlby, J. (1988) *A Secure Base: Clinical Applications of Attachment Theory*. London: Routledge.

Campbell, B. (1993) *Goliath: Britain's Dangerous Places*. London: Methuen.

Chapman, T. and Hough, M. (1998) *Evidence Based Practice: A Guide to Effective Practice*. London: Home Office.

Children (NI) order (1995). Belfast: HMSO.

Coomaraswamy, R. (1998) Statement by UN Special Rapporteur on 'Violence against women, its causes and consequences'.

Corrigan, S. (1999) 'Caught in the middle – exploring children's and young people's experiences of domestic violence.' *Child Care in Practice 5*, 1.

Courtney, A. (1997) 'Why domestic violence matters.' In *When Home is Where the Hurt Is*. Belfast Conference of Religions of Ireland.

Covey, S. (1992) *The Seven Habits of Highly Effective People*. London: Simon and Schuster.

Covey, S. (1999) *The 7 Habits of Highly Effective Families*. London: Simon and Schuster.

Craze, R. (1998) *Relaxation*. London: Hodder and Stoughton.

Cummings, E.M. and Davies, P. (1994) *Children and Marital Conflict.* London: Simon and Schuster.

Daft, R.L. (1995) *Organisation Theory and Design.* St Paul: West Publishing Company.

David, D. and Brannon, R. (eds) (1976) *The Forty-Nine Percent Majority.* Reading, Mass.: Addison-Wesley.

Dept of Economic Development (1999) 'Tackling violence against women.' A consultation paper. Belfast: DED.

DHSS and NIO (1995) *Tackling Domestic Violence: A Policy for Northern Ireland.* Belfast: NIO.

Dobash, R.E. and Dobash, R. (1992) *Women, Violence and Social Change.* London: Routledge.

Dobash, R., Dobash, R.E., Cavanagh, K. and Lewis, R. (1996) *Research Evaluation Programmes of Violent Men.* Edinburgh: HMSO.

Edleson, J.L. and Tolman, R.M. (1992) *Intervention for Men who Batter.* London: Sage.

Egan, G. (1995) *The Skilled Helper.* California: Brooks/Cole.

Emerge (1997) *Counselling and Education to Stop Domestic Violence.* Mass.: Cambridge.

Farrington, D. and West, D. (1990) 'The Cambridge study in delinquent development: a long-term follow-up of 411 London males.' In H. Kerner and G. Kaiser (eds) *Criminality: Personality, Behaviour and Life History.* Berlin: Springer-Verlag.

Freire, P. (1976) *Education – The Practice of Freedom.* London: Writers and Readers.

Gillette, D. (1992) 'Men and intimacy.' In C. Harding (ed) *Wingspan: Inside the Men's Movement.* New York: St Martin's Press.

Goddard, C.R. and Hiller, P.C. (1993) 'Child sexual abuse: assault in a violent context.' *Australian Journal of Social Issues 28*, 1, 20–33.

Goldman, D. (1996) *Emotional Intelligence: Why It Can Matter More Than IQ.* London: Bloomsbury.

Gondolf, E.W. (1997) 'Batterer programs: what we know and need to know.' *Journal of Interpersonal Violence 12*, 1.

Goodman, M.S. and Fallon, B.C. (1995) *Pattern Changing for Abused Women.* London: Sage.

Gottman, J. *et al.* (1995) 'The relationship between heart rate, reactivity, emotionally aggressive behaviour, and general violence in batterers.' *Journal of Female Psychology 9*, 227–228.

Gray, J. (1992) *Men are from Mars. Women are from Venus.* New York: Harper Collins.

Gulbenkian Foundation (1995) *Children and Violence.* London: Calouste.

Hammer, J. (1999) Unpublished paper presented at Northern Ireland Women's Aid Conference. Derry.

Hardiman, M. (2000) *Ordinary Heroes: A Future For Men*. Dublin: Gill and Macmillan Ltd.

Hart, B. (1993) 'Battered women and the criminal justice system.' *American Behavioural Scientist 36*, 5, 624–638.

Hart, B. (1994) 'Lethality and dangerous assessments.' *Violence Update 4*, 10, 7–8.

Honey, P. (1994) *Learning Log. A Way to Enhance Learning from Experience*. Berkshire: P. Honey.

Hotaling, G.T. and Sugerman, D.B. (1986) 'Analysis of risk markers in husband to wife violence.' *Violence and Victims 1*, 101–124.

Hoyle, C. (1998) *Negotiating Domestic Violence: Police, Criminal Justice and Victims*. Oxford: Oxford University Press.

Jacobson, N.S. *et al.* (1994) 'Affect. Verbal content and psychophysiology in the arguments of couples with a violent husband.' *Journal of Clinical and Consulting Psychology*. July.

Kelly, L. (1999) *Domestic Violence Matters: An Evaluation of a Development Project*. London: Home Office.

Kilmartin, C.T. (1994) *The Masculine Self*. Toronto: Maxwell Macmillan.

Kolb, D.A. (1984) *Experiential Learning: Experiences as the Source of Learning Development*. New Jersey: Prentice Hall.

Lloyd, T. (1996) 'The role of training in the development of work with men.' In T. Newburn and G. Mair *Working with Men*. Dorset: Russell House.

McWilliams, M. (1999) Quoted in *Belfast Telegraph* 1 November 1999.

McWilliams, M. and McKiernan, J. (1993) *Bringing it Out in the Open: Domestic Violence in Northern Ireland*. Belfast: HMSO.

McWilliams, M. and Spence, L. (1996) *Taking Domestic Violence Seriously: Issues for the Civil and Criminal Justice System*. Belfast: Stationery Office.

Maguire, J. (ed) (1995) *What Works: Reducing Re-Offending*. Guidelines from research and practice. Chichester: John Wiley and Sons.

Manalive (1990) *Men's Programme*. California.

Miedzian, M. (1992) *Boys will be Boys*. London: Virago.

Miller, W.R. and Rollnick, S. (1991) *Motivational Interviewing: Preparing People to Change Addictive Behaviours*. New York: Guildford Publishers.

Mirrlees-Black, C. (1999) *Domestic Violence: Findings from a New British Crime Survey Self-Completion Questionnaire*. London: Home Office.

Morran, D. and Wilson, M. (1997) *Men who are Violent to Women: A Group Practice Manual.* Dorset: Russell House.

Morran, D. and Wilson, M. (1999) 'Working with men who are violent to partners: striving for good practice.' In H. Kemshall and J. Pritchard *Good Practice in Working with Violence.* London: Jessica Kingsley.

Mullender, A. (1996) *Rethinking Domestic Violence: The Social Work and Probation Response.* London: Routledge.

Mullender, A. and Morley, R. (eds) (1994) *Children Living Through Domestic Violence: Putting Men's Abuse of Women on the Child Care Agenda.* London: Whiting Birch.

Murphy, K. (1996) 'Men and offending groups.' In T. Newburn and G. Mair *Working with Men.* Dorset: Russell House.

Nasher, F.B. and Mehrtens, S.E. (1993) *What's Really Going On?* Chicago: Corporantes.

Novacco, R. (1976) 'The functions and regulation of the arousal of anger.' *American Journal of Psychiatry 133*, 10.

O'Hagan, K. (1997) 'The problem of engaging men in child protection work.' *British Journal of Social Work 27*, 25–42.

Patrick, C. *et al.* (1994) 'Emotion in the criminal psychopath: fear image processing.' *Journal of Abnormal Psychology 103.*

Peck, M.S. (1983) *The Road Less Travelled.* London: Hutchinson and Co.

Pence, E. and Paymar, M. (1993) *Education Groups for Men Who Batter: The Duluth Model.* New York: Springer.

Pinker, S. (1997) *How the Mind Works.* London: Penguin.

Prochaska, J. and Di Clemente, C. (1984) *The Transtheoretical Approach: Crossing Traditional Boundaries of Therapy.* Homewood: Dow Jones Irwin.

Rice, M.E. (1997) 'Violent offender research and implications for the criminal justice system.' *American Psychologist 52*, 4, 414–423.

Rosenfeld, B. (1992) 'Court ordered treatment of spouse abuse.' *Clinical Psychology Review 12*, 205–226.

Routledge, P. (1997) *John Hume: A Biography.* London: HarperCollins.

Russell, M.N. (1995) *Confronting Abusive Beliefs: Group Treatment for Abusive Men.* London: Sage.

Sheehy, G. (1996) *New Passages: Mapping Your Life across Time.* London: HarperCollins.

Sheehy, G. (1998) *Passages in Men's Lives.* London: Simon and Schuster.

Straus, M.A. and Gelles, R.J. (1990) *Physical Violence in American Families: Risk Factors and Adaptations to Violence in 8145 Families.* New Brunswick, NJ: Tranaction Publishers.

Thompson, N. (1995) *Theory and Practice in Health and Social Welfare*. Buckingham: Open University Press.

Walker, L. (1979) *The Battered Woman*. New York: Harper and Row.

Waring, T.H. and Wilson, J. (1990) *Be Safe: A Self Help Manual for Domestic Violence*. Bolton: Hardman & Co.

Wilkinson, H. and Mulgan, G. (1995) *Freedom's Children: Work, Relationships, and Politics for 18–34 Year Olds Today*. London: Denos.

Woodcock, M. and Frances, D. (1992) *Implementing Change*. Hampshire: Connaught Training Ltd.

Worthington, T. (1998) Opening address to 'Working Together', Regional Forum on Domestic Violence (NI).

Wrangham, R. and Peterson, D. (1997) *Demonic Males: Apes and the Origins of Human Violence*. London: Bloomsbury.

Zehr, H. (1995) *A New Focus for Crime and Justice: Changing Lenses*. Ontario: Herald Press.

Subject Index

Author Index